Oct 1990.

To Gan,

Many Happy Returns
Lots of love

Joyce xx

Queen Mother
THE LICHFIELD SELECTION

Queen Mother

THE LICHFIELD SELECTION

A Visual Record of Ninety Remarkable Years
Selected from the Archives of the Hulton-Deutsch Collection
by **The Earl of Lichfield**

DOUBLEDAY
LONDON – NEW YORK – TORONTO – SYDNEY – AUKLAND

Frontispiece: Queen Elizabeth during her tour of Canada in 1989.
Title page: The Duchess of York with Princesses Elizabeth and
Margaret at Royal Lodge, Windsor, in June 1936.

© Berkswell Publishing Co Ltd 1990
Produced by John Stidolph
Edited by Charles Jacoby
Designed by Paul Watkins

First published in 1990 by DOUBLEDAY
a division of Transworld Publishers Ltd
61–63 Uxbridge Road, London W5 5SA

DOUBLEDAY, a division of Bantam Doubleday Dell
Publishing Group Inc. 666 Fifth Avenue,
New York, New York 10103.

DOUBLEDAY CANADA LTD
105 Bond Street, Toronto, Ontario

TRANSWORLD PUBLISHERS (AUSTRALIA) PTY LTD
15–23 Helles Avenue, Moorebank, NSW 2170

TRANSWORLD PUBLISHERS (NZ) LTD
Cnr Moselle and Waipareira Aves, Henderson, Auckland

British Library Cataloguing in Publication Data applied for

Typeset by Footnote Graphics, Warminster
Originated by J. Film, Bangkok
Printed in Italy by New Interlitho

ISBN 0 385 400616

CONTENTS

1900·1923
LADY ELIZABETH

QUEEN ELIZABETH was born the Hon. Elizabeth Bowes-Lyon in London on 4th August 1900. Her birth certificate says St Paul's Walden Bury, the family home in Hertfordshire, but that was a mistake made by her father, my great grandfather, Lord Glamis, who was fined 7/6d for registering the birth late. She was the youngest but one of ten children of whom eight survived until the First World War.

The Lyons are amongst the oldest and most distinguished Scottish families. Sir John Lyon had been given Glamis in 1372 by Robert II of Scotland. They have always had nationalist tendencies and supported the Jacobite cause during the 18th century. However, in 1767 Lord Glamis married an heiress named Mary Bowes from Durham, my great-great-great-great grandmother, and adopted her name. She brought with her the St Paul's Walden Bury estate, which anglicized the family. For a while they were the Lyon-Bowes, but Queen Elizabeth's grandfather changed the name around to its present form. It was between the two great houses, and 20 St James's Square in London that the girl who was to become Britain's last empress grew up.

Chips Channon, the politician and diarist, called Glamis Castle 'sinister and lugubrious'. The Bowes-Lyons spent a three month summer holiday there every year. Days were spent playing cricket or tennis, both of which the family were keen on. According to Michael Bowes-Lyon, one of Queen Elizabeth's brothers, there was 'one special umpire, Mr Arthur Fossett, short, round, red-faced and fat, who was trained never to no-ball father and always to give his appeals out'. There was also shooting, which Queen Elizabeth has never taken to, even though her husband was a good shot. For those who didn't shoot there was salmon fishing on the River Tay, and that is still one of Queen Elizabeth's greatest loves. After supper the family and guests enjoyed games of charades in the great hall in front of the fire, and dancing and singing to the Countess of Strathmore playing the piano. The Bowes-Lyon children were encouraged to play host whenever possible. While her husband was in the Antarctic, Lady Scott wrote to him mentioning 'little Lady Elizabeth Lyon' who took her on a tour of the Castle. Lady Elizabeth was good at this. 'Shall us sit and talk?' she is remembered saying to wallflowers at house parties.

At the age of twelve Lady Elizabeth had her portrait painted by Miss E. Gertrude Thomson. She asked the artist whether she had ever seen any ghosts. When she learnt that Miss Thomson hadn't she confided, 'I haven't seen them yet, but someday I may'. Glamis Castle is one of the most haunted in Scotland, and at night it looks positively chilling. A tongueless and handless woman is said to run bleeding across the park at midnight. She had been punished by the family for coming across a dreadful secret. There is Lord Crawford who had been thrown down some stone stairs by Lord Glamis in 1486 after a quarrel over a game of cards. It was the early hours of Sunday morning, and thus a sacrilege. Beardie Crawford said that he would carry on playing with the Devil if he wanted to. He has since appeared to children, who complain of a gross bearded figure bending over them in bed, and Lord Halifax swore that Beardie haunted the Blue Room. There is a vaporous white lady and, until it was turned into a bathroom, the small room adjoining Lady Elizabeth's room used to have its bed mysteriously stripped at night. In the same vein there is a door which however tightly wedged shut at night was always open by morning.

St Paul's Walden Bury, north of Hatfield was a much happier place. It is a redbrick Queen Anne house built by Sir William Chambers, covered in honeysuckle and magnolia, set on a slight rise, and surrounded by lawns and woodland, making it remarkably tranquil in that busy county. Here, Lady Elizabeth learnt to ride on her Shetland pony Bobs, who was even allowed into the house. There was a fleahouse with a ladder so rickety that no nurse or governess could ever climb it. There Lady Elizabeth and her younger brother David would go to play truant from their governesses. They hoarded fruit, chocolate and Woodbines up there, though the cigarettes were unsmoked. They were for a future experiment which is still indefinitely postponed.

The children were in the care of their nurse, Clara Knight, for the first years, though their mother taught them to read and write. As David later mentioned, 'At the ages of six and seven we could each of us have written a fairly detailed account of all the Bible stories'. Religion was important to the Bowes-Lyons. The chapel at Glamis Castle was used for morning prayers. The family motto was taken seriously: 'In Thee, O Lord, have I put my trust.'

Mademoiselle Lang was the first governess. She remembered meeting Lady Elizabeth for the first time: 'an enchanting child with tiny hands and feet and rose-petal colouring, murmuring with perfect politeness, "I do hope you will be happy here".' The Countess of Strathmore, Lady Elizabeth's mother, sat in on these early lessons. Mademoiselle Lang left after David had gone to a prep school in Broadstairs on the South Coast. Meanwhile Lady Elizabeth endured two terms of a day school in South Kensington run by the Misses Birtwhistle, who had vague feminist tendencies. When that didn't work, Fraulein Kathie Kuebler from Germany was brought in with a more strict regime of lessons, culminating in the Junior Oxford Exam which Lady Elizabeth passed. Kathie also took charge of her at some of the young peoples' dances which were taking place. At one of them Lady Elizabeth danced with Prince Albert, her future husband. Most significantly she was allowed to have lunch with her parents at the unusually young age of thirteen. There she met notables such as Viscount Goschen, future Viceroy of India, Lord Hamilton, Lord Rosebery, Lord Curzon and Lord Lansdowne who were amongst the most influential politicians of their age.

The day after Lady Elizabeth's fourteenth birthday, Britain declared war on Germany. Kathie had gone back to Germany for her parents' silver wedding celebrations, and never returned. There was excitement as two of Lady Elizabeth's brothers, Fergus and my grandfather, Jock, were married that autumn. Then there was knitting, shirt-making and sleeping-bag stuffing for the 5th Black Watch, the local battalion. Glamis was turned into a hospital for the wounded. Lady Elizabeth had many new responsibilities while her sister Lady Rose undertook training as a nurse in London, though on her return to help at Glamis, Lady Elizabeth was relegated once more to the schoolroom. She assumed responsibility for the household in 1915 when the Countess of Strathmore learnt that Fergus had been killed. In 1910 Lady Elizabeth's elder brother Alec had died at the age of twenty-four, which gave her a sense of the desolation of death. Then in 1916 another of those terrible telegrams arrived, announcing that brother Michael was missing. Luckily he turned out to be a prisoner, though he had been shot in the head and was too ill to communicate. With Scottish second-sight David had maintained that this was the case all along, and had refused to wear the black armband of mourning. Even after the Armistice Glamis Castle continued to be a hospital, until in 1919 all the wounded had left. Meanwhile, Lady Elizabeth started out in society.

'Elizabeth Lyon is out now and Cecilia had a dance for her. How many hearts Elizabeth will break,' wrote Lady Buxton. Apparently Lady Elizabeth had a feverish temperature on the day of her coming-out dance in 1919. It was the heyday of an age when debutantes were still presented to the King and Queen at Court. Lady Lavinia Spencer, the Princess of Wales's great aunt, married Lord Annaly in April, and Lady Elizabeth was a bridesmaid. There was Ascot week and Goodwood and a blossoming friendship with Princess Mary through Lady Airlie. In 1920 the Forfar Ball took place at Glamis Castle. Lord Strathmore was Lord Lieutenant for Forfarshire, later Angus. Among other fashionable parties there was the Royal Air Force Ball at the Ritz, and Lord Farquhar's dance.

Lady Elizabeth could have met Prince Albert almost anywhere. That summer he visited Glamis from Balmoral, taking in Cortachy Castle, the Airlies' seat, where Princess Mary was staying. Over the next two years their friendship grew. Then in January 1923 he wooed her with a platinum ring set with a Kashmir sapphire and two diamonds, and she accepted him. As Chips Channon put it: 'There's not a man in England today who doesn't envy him. The clubs are in gloom.'

The wedding took place in April. It wasn't broadcast to the nation, because it was feared that it might be listened to in pubs, or heard by men who hadn't removed their hats. The couple had their honeymoon at Polesden Lacey in Surrey, the home of Mrs Greville, a royal family friend. On the third day of their stay it was announced in the *London Gazette* that Lady Elizabeth should now be known as Her Royal Highness the Duchess of York.

This is one of the earliest known pictures of the Hon. Elizabeth Bowes-Lyon, taken in 1902. Despite the highly stylized pose it is clear that she possessed remarkable poise and charm, even at the age of two. She drew this from both her parents. Her modesty came from her father, who was a quiet old-fashioned landowner, and her confidence and fortitude from her mother, who was born a Cavendish-Bentinck and was a highly talented musician. It is a shame that we cannot see more of the painted background in the picture, so typical of turn-of-the-century photographs, and later adopted by Cecil Beaton. However, the flowers are an accurate prediction of things to come. You can see a prop by her left hand, enabling her to keep still enough for the slow shutter speed.

Page 6: This hand-tinted black-and-white picture came from a 1921 society magazine. Colour film was still extremely primitive. At that time Lady Elizabeth was being invited to all the parties, but contemporaries noted that she wasn't really of the cigarette-and-cocktail set at all. Lady Asquith saw a 'look of experience beyond her years' on her face. This was a look born from the terrible war, which some magazines were still referring to as That Great Adventure. It had taught Britain's bright young things unknown hardship, and in the early 1920s most wanted to cram in all the experiences of growing up that they felt they had missed. However, Lady Elizabeth did not feel the need to be as wild as many of her contemporaries. Perhaps because she had already undertaken considerable responsibility.

Eyes wide open, this is a heavenly picture of four-year-old Elizabeth taken in daylight. The flowering twigs suggest that it was spring, though they could be silk. Later that year her grandfather died, her father became 14th Earl of Strathmore, and Elizabeth adopted the courtesy title of Lady. At this stage in her life she hardly knew of the city, except as a place to which her senior siblings would disappear. Mary, her eldest surviving sister, was twenty-one years old in 1904. St Paul's Walden Bury was Elizabeth's whole world. In the late 1920s, Lady Cynthia Asquith related stories of Lady Elizabeth's early life, as told by the then Duchess of York herself: 'At the bottom of the garden, where the sun always seems to be shining, is *the wood* – the haunt of fairies, with its anemones and ponds, and moss grown statues, and the *big oak* under which she reads and where the two ring doves, Caroline-Curly-Love and Rhoda-Wrigley-Worm, contentedly coo in their wicker-work "Ideal Home".'

Opposite: This portrait of Lady Elizabeth with her younger brother David was taken in 1909 at Glamis Castle. She is dressed as a princess and he as a jester for a dancing lesson under their venerable instructor Mr Neal. The Bowes-Lyons were the last Scottish family to maintain a full-time jester. The inseparable pair, who were referred to as the Two Benjamins by their mother, lived under the care of, first, their nurse Clara Knight, known as Allah, then a French governess, followed by a German, Fräulein Kuebler. Glamis Castle was always associated with holidays, when the family, pets and staff would take the Flying Scotsman 400 miles northwards. David and Elizabeth would play games of defending the castle by pouring 'boiling oil' on 'raiders'. Visitors were thus frequently drenched with cold water.

The Glamis household threw itself into the war effort. This is Lady Elizabeth running a stall at a charity sale in 1915. The Castle became a convalescent hospital for the wounded. Lady Elizabeth looked after her charges assiduously, making forays to the local stores to buy their tobacco and other requirements. When her brother Fergus was killed at the Battle of Loos in 1915 she had to manage the household as well, while her mother retired to her room. In December 1916 she alerted everyone to a fire which swept the central keep. She organized chains of people to hand down the furniture and pictures away from the blaze. However, the indomitable sense of humour was often present. She dressed her brother David as a young lady of fashion and introduced him to the soldiers as her cousin. Men from all over the Empire grew well under her care, and on future royal tours of Canada and Australia she would always take the time to meet or ask after them.

Eventually the memory of war began to fade, and there was great public celebration when at the end of November 1921 the engagement was announced between Princess Mary and Lord Lascelles. It was the first royal wedding since the War and was granted the status of a state ceremonial. Lady Elizabeth, along with Lady Mary Cambridge, Lady May Cambridge, Lady Mary Thynne and the Hon. Diamond Hardinge, were bridesmaids, and in February 1922 they processed in carriages to Westminster Abbey. All these other girls were to be bridesmaids to Lady Elizabeth a little over a year later. Lady Elizabeth had met Princess Mary through their mutual involvement in the Girl Guide movement, this was the first time that the press took any interest in her, and it gave her some idea of the form her own wedding would take. Her dress is typical of the age, though more ornate than those of her own bridesmaids.

This picture was taken at Glamis during the summer of 1922, by which time Prince Albert had started his courtship of Lady Elizabeth. However it was not until the following January, when the Prince was a guest for the week-end at St Paul's Walden Bury, that he asked Lady Elizabeth to marry him, and whether she had refused him before or not, this time she accepted him. 'All right – Bertie', read the pre-arranged telegram which he sent to his parents at Sandringham. In 1921 King George V had written: 'You will be a lucky fellow if she accepts you', and he couldn't hide his delight now. Queen Mary, later on in 1921, had called her 'the one girl who could made Bertie happy', and she too was pleased.

Opposite: Various portraits were taken during the months before the wedding. This is one of the least affected, perhaps reminiscent of Lord Snowdon's work today. The stage backdrops of her childhood have disappeared to make everything in the picture uncomplicated. The style hasn't quite settled down, though. The romantic element is injected with the use of the soft focus, but unfortunately the retouching is just too heavy. The girlish fringe is still there, though that was removed shortly afterwards. In classic 1920s style the pearls offset the dress. The simplicity of the technique saves this picture from her strict pose.

Left: Lady Elizabeth is walking in front of Glamis Castle with her mother, my great grandmother, early in 1923. The Countess of Strathmore was born Nina Cecilia Cavendish-Bentinck in 1862, great granddaughter of the 3rd Duke of Portland, who was prime minister under George III. She would have succeeded as Duke if she had been a boy. She was an extraordinarily good painter, and she played the piano, both of which accomplishments sparked her daughter's interest in the arts. She planned the Glamis Castle gardens and tirelessly supervised their growth. Both Queen Elizabeth and her younger brother David have been past presidents of the Royal Horticultural Society. Celia, as she was known, was also an accomplished hostess with the gift of making any guest feel at ease. It seems that all these attributes have been visited upon her daughter.

Opposite: In 1921 Lady Elizabeth became district commissioner of the Glamis and Easshire Parish Girl Guides, thus demonstrating her early commitment to public service. Princess Mary, later the Princess Royal, who was three years older than Lady Elizabeth was also interested in the Guide movement and the two became close friends. They originally met through Mabell, Countess of Airlie, who lived in Airlie Castle near Glamis, and Princess Mary later came to inspect the Forfarshire Guides. Lady Elizabeth was a bridesmaid at her wedding in 1922. At that time Lady Elizabeth's romance with the Duke of York had hardly started. In this heavily posed picture of 1923 she is being presented with a wedding gift by a group of her guides.

Left: On the left is my great uncle, Lord Glamis, and on the right my great grandfather, Lord Strathmore. This picture was taken during the months before the wedding, and is notable because the subjects look so relaxed. Incidentally, the old Earl was extremely fond of his moustache. He used to make a show of parting it in order to kiss his younger children. He was a fine cricketer and an expert shot, and he enjoyed drinking cocoa for breakfast. Patrick, Lord Glamis, Lady Elizabeth's elder brother, had survived the war in the Scots Guards. He was sixteen years older than her and had married Lady Dorothy Osborne, daughter of the Duke of Leeds, in 1914, and she had borne him an heir, Timothy, in 1918.

Opposite: On 18th March 1923 the Duke and Duchess of York went together to McVitie & Price in Edinburgh to see their wedding cake under construction. It was finally to stand nine feet high and weigh 800 pounds. It consisted of four tiers; the first decorated with their combined arms, then the Strathmore arms, the arms of York, and the top, which was shaped like a castle, bore a vase of white flowers. Gold charms were stirred into the mixture and baked in the cake. The girl on the left is clearly more interested in the camera.

On 26th April 1923, for the last time as a single woman, Lady Elizabeth stepped out of her family house at 17 Bruton Street, Mayfair, on her way to her wedding. A footman stands on either side of her, and her father, Lord Strathmore, my great grandfather, is out of the picture waiting in the state landau. Her flowers were also in the carriage. They included sprigs of white heather from Scotland, and white roses to signify the Duchy of York. As she entered Westminster Abbey she placed them on the tomb of the unknown soldier. The uniforms in this picture are of great interest. The royal coachmen are magnificent in their greatcoats and hats, and the footmen are sporting the livery of the Strathmores.

Below: The Duke and Duchess of York stand surrounded by bridesmaids and train-bearers in the Throne Room at Buckingham Palace after their wedding. The bridesmaids at the back are Lady Mary Cambridge on the left and her cousin Lady May Cambridge on the right. Lady Mary's parents were Adolphus, Duke of Teck, and Lady Margaret Grosvenor, the fourth daughter of the 1st Duke of Westminster. Lady Mary married the Duke of Beaufort later in 1923 and is now the dowager Duchess. The Beauforts host the Badminton horse trials to which Queen Elizabeth is still a regular visitor. Lady May, whose parents were Alexander Earl of Athlone and Princess Alice of Albany, married Sir Henry Abel Smith, who became Governor of Queensland. The Duke and his bride were to visit them on trips to Australia. Seated from left to right are the Hon. Diamond Hardinge, Lady Mary Thynne, Lady Katharine Hamilton and Miss Elizabeth Cator. Betty Cator went on to marry one of Lady Elizabeth's elder brothers, Michael, my great uncle. The two girls knew each other from the short time that they suffered together at the Misses Birtwhistles' Academy in Sloane Street. Lady Mary Thynne, once described by *The Tatler* as 'the lovely Bath girl', married an Alexander. Lady Katharine Hamilton, a great aunt of the present Princess of Wales, married Lt. Col. Sir Reginald Seymour in 1930, who died in 1938. She was a Woman of the Bedchamber to Queen Mary from 1927 to 1930 and to Queen Elizabeth from 1937

to 1960. She became a DCVO in 1961. Diamond, daughter of Lord Hardinge of Penshurst who was ambassador to France, married Captain Abercrombie, but died only a few years later after an operation. The two girls kneeling, the train bearers, both aged eleven, are the Hon. Elizabeth Elphinstone and the Hon. Cecilia Bowes-Lyon. Elizabeth Elphinstone was the Duchess's niece. Her parents were the 16th Baron Elphinstone and Mary, Lady Elizabeth's sister. Cecilia was another niece, the daughter of elder brother Patrick, Lord Glamis. The bridesmaids wore ivory georgette and Nottingham lace with a green tulle sash fastened by a silver thistle and white rose. The bride wore ivory chiffon moire with pearls and silver thread. Her sleeves were of Nottingham lace, and the train, which used to be her mother's, was of point de Flandres lace on tulle. The Duke wore the uniform of a group captain in the Royal Air Force, with Garter riband and star, and Thistle star.

After the wedding the newly married couple made an appearance on the balcony at Buckingham Palace. The heavy crimson drape gives the picture a slightly funereal air. This photograph must have been taken from scaffolding in front and slightly to the right of the Palace, not from the Victoria Memorial (the 'Wedding Cake'), as would be the case today. The fashion element is notable. The younger members of the royal family are beginning to adopt the styles of the 1920s. From left to right are Princess Mary, Princess Maud, Queen Alexandra, Queen Mary, the bride and groom, and King George V. Princess Mary had married Viscount Lascelles only the year before. He became the 6th Earl of Harewood, and in 1932 the King bestowed on her the further style of Princess Royal. She died in 1965. Princess Maud was the daughter of the previous Princess Royal, and granddaughter of King Edward VII and Queen Alexandra. She married Lord Carnegie later in 1923 and he went on to become 11th Earl of Southesk.

1923-1936
DUCHESS OF YORK

'If she weren't late she would be perfect,
and how horrible that would be'
King George V

THE second half of the Yorks' honeymoon was at Glamis Castle where the Duchess caught whooping cough. '*So* unromantic', she wrote to Queen Mary. After this they moved to their new home, White Lodge in Richmond Park, which had been built by King George II as a 'place of refreshment after the chase'. It was in many ways inconvenient. Not only was it too far from the York's increasing duties in London – in fact they used 17 Bruton Street almost as much, and their chauffeur once lost himself in the pea-soup fog which descended over the park – but also trippers were constantly peering at them through the gates. However, they set to and revived the large garden. On one occasion the Duke's legs were discovered by Queen Mary sticking out from under a mass of vegetation. When his muddy face appeared she made him stay while she went to fetch a camera. A telling sentence he wrote to his mother in April 1924 reads: 'The boiler is actually finished, and marvel of marvels worked on Sunday.' They had no permanent country base until in 1931 the King gave them Royal Lodge, near Windsor, which had previously been inhabited by the Duke of Cumberland, known as the Butcher of Culloden, and the Prince Regent, and took a year to renovate.

The Duchess immediately began on the duties of royal life. Princess Christian, Queen Victoria's third daughter, had recently died at the age of seventy-seven leaving several charities patronless. The Duchess took on most of them. She also asked whether there was any possibility of a serious tour of the Dominions, but the King deemed that the couple should be given time to settle down. The opportunity to represent their country soon came to the Yorks though. Shortly after her first public appearance, at the Hendon Air Show, she and her husband were chosen to become godparents of King Alexander of Yugoslavia's first son and heir. Lord Curzon, the Foreign Secretary, advised them to accept, so they quickly packed and left for Belgrade. 'Curzon should be drowned for giving such short notice', wrote the Duke to his comptroller Louis Greig.

In late 1924 they went to Northern Ireland, and the Duke wrote of his wife: 'Elizabeth has been marvellous as usual, the people simply love her already.' The six counties and parliament had been recognized by the Government of Ireland Act of 1920, and this was the first royal visit to the province since King George V had inaugurated its parliament in 1921. Then the Yorks went to East Africa.

Their first stop, having travelled via Marseilles and Mombasa aboard the liner *Mulbera*, was Nairobi. The Governor Sir Robert Coryndon had them to stay for Christmas, and after the new year they went on safari. The Duchess shot well with her .275 Rigby, but was more keen to take photographs. During a stay with Francis Lord Scott at Rongai they heard of the death of Sir Robert Coryndon after an operation, so the Duke cut short his exploits in the bush to go to the funeral in Nairobi. In Uganda, which was the next stop, the Duchess shot crocodiles. They journeyed down the White Nile, and the Duke had his first elephant, whose tusks weighed ninety pounds each. The ivory later stood proudly in the hall of their house in Piccadilly. The royal party slept out on the deck of their paddle-steamer the *Samuel Baker*, despite the mosquitoes, to escape the oven-like lower decks. Their official duties throughout included the colourful ceremonies of meeting the headmen of tribes. In Talodi they watched a march-past of 12,000 Nubian warriors. Along the Upper Nile the Duchess spent one night in a tent which collapsed twice in the torrential rain. On arrival at the Port of Sudan they boarded the liner *Maloja* for home.

After the birth of Princess Elizabeth, and before the Yorks were sent on a world tour, a Harley Street speech therapist called Lionel Logue was called in to help the Duke with his stammer. Logue was born in 1880 in South Australia, and had always wanted to be a doctor. However, he couldn't bear the sight of blood so he set up a school of elocution in Perth, working particularly well with shell-shocked soldiers. The Duke had been to therapists but without success, so he was reluctant to put himself in the hands of another. However, Logue's method of teaching his patients an entirely new way of breathing had a good effect. The Duke was not perfect, but he was capable of speeches without pauses. It was mostly a question of confidence. Logue was employed by the Duke throughout his life, and when, as King George VI, he was being treated for the lung cancer that finally killed him, his physician Price Thomas asked if he always breathed in this way: 'I was taught to breathe that way in 1926, and I've gone on doing so'. 'Another feather in your cap, you see', he then wrote to Logue.

The tour of the Dominions began in January 1927. The Yorks sailed to New Zealand via Las Palmas in the Canary Islands, Puerto Rica, Kingston in Jamaica, the Panama Canal, Nukuhiva in the Marquesas Islands, and Suva in Fiji. They crossed the line on the 24th, and the Duke was dunked in the water by a character dressed as Neptune, while the Duchess was awarded the spurious Most Maritime Order of the Golden Mermaid. They were a huge success in both North and South Island, though unfortunately the Duchess caught tonsillitis and spent some time recuperating in the Commercial Hotel in Nelson, before being advised by doctors to return to Government House in Wellington. While she was in Nelson, a sign was put up outside the hotel asking motorists not to hoot when they drove past. This was adhered to with great enthusiasm, for the Antipodeans loved her. A special force of seventy-six policemen, with an average height of six foot three inches, was assigned to her.

In Australia the Yorks were in Melbourne for Anzac Day where they reviewed 25,000 servicemen, and before going walkabout in the bush, the Duke successfully opened the new parliament building in Canberra. The Australians were not expecting him to live up to the stylish Prince of Wales, who had toured Australia in 1920, but his rumoured inability to speak proved largely untrue, and they saw in him a man who was trying hard to do his job, which is something Australians always admire. Sir Tom Bridges, Governor of South Australia wrote to the King of them: 'His Royal Highness has touched people profoundly by his youth, his simplicity and natural bearing, while the Duchess has had a tremendous ovation and leaves us with the responsibility of having a continent in love with her. The visit has done untold good.' On 23rd May they went back to England with thirty tons of gifts, and despite a fire in the boiler room whilst crossing the Indian Ocean, they reached their first stop of Mauritius. 'Did you ever realize Ma'am, that at one time it was pretty bad?' asked the Captain. 'Yes I did', she replied. 'Every hour someone came and told me that it was nothing to worry about, so I knew there was real trouble.' After that it was Malta, Gibraltar, and finally the welcoming arms of Princess Elizabeth at Buckingham Palace.

In 1924 145 Piccadilly became vacant. It was exactly what the Duchess of York had been looking for, and even better, it belonged to the Crown Estates. It was finally ready to move into after the world tour, though Princess Elizabeth and her nanny, the Duchess's old nanny Allah, had arrived a week before to settle in. It was to be their home until the abdication less than ten years later, which was the only period that they were ever able to enjoy anything approaching family life. To that end there were no foreign tours until after the Duke's accession. The first pet they brought in was a parrot called Jimmie given to them by a working mens' club down under. 'Jimmie have a drink!' it would squawk in a rich Australian brogue.

The birth of their children did not stir the nation to any great extent for the Duke was not expected to ascend to the throne. Princess Margaret, arrived in 1930. The Duke left the children's upbringing to their mother. He had had a comparatively harsh childhood, and by no means wished to see the same inflicted on his daughters. Later he wrote: 'I have watched you grow up all these years with pride under the skilful direction of Mama who, as you know, is the most marvellous person in the world in my eyes.' Their early education was much the same as their mother's. They were read stories from The Bible, and played games of mime. Their pocket money was limited; not quite as stringently as their mother's had been – a famous telegram of hers to her father read 'SOS LSD RSVP' – but enough to stop them becoming complacent. Their Uncle David, the Prince of Wales, who had also suffered the strictures of a royal childhood, would occasionally call and play games of Racing Demon and Snap.

The Prince of Wales had had a number of liaisons with ladies, including Winifred Dudley Ward and Thelma Lady Furness. However, in 1932 he invited the American Wallis Simpson and her husband to his country house Fort Belvedere in Sunningdale, Berkshire, for the weekend. It was there that their affair really started. The Yorks were indifferent to her, until the Duke's brother became King, when they began to realize what an influence she exercised over him. After the abdication, the Duchess of Windsor, as Wallis became, appeared to conduct a kind of war of attrition against Queen Elizabeth which only seemed to be brought to an end at last at the Duke of Windsor's funeral in 1972. Although I must say that when I photographed the Duke and Duchess in Paris, once we had broken the rather formal ice, they could not have been more charming.

The Duchess of York spent Christmas 1935 ill in bed at Royal Lodge. Queen Mary asked the Duke to come to Sandringham because the King was also ill and she needed help with the house party. He returned to the Lodge after three days with the news that the King might not live. He was recalled to Sandringham almost at once, but arrived only in time to see his father's life finally ebb away.

The new King was Edward VIII. At first he was conscientious in his duties. To begin with official papers were signed promptly, and even had notes pencilled into the margin, but after a while they came back marked with the rings from the bottom of a cocktail glass, and at longer and longer intervals. He became indiscreet over Wallis Simpson. By today's standards the British press were unimaginably kind to him. Hardly a word came out until the end, even though in America and on the Continent the affair was headline news. There was a famous picture of the King rowing a boat alone around the yacht *Nahlin*, which he had borrowed from Lady Yule to cruise the Dalmatian Coast. Newspapers which used the same photograph abroad showed that Mrs Simpson was sitting in the back.

On 10th December 1937 he signed. 'I, Edward the Eighth, of Great Britain, Ireland, and the British Dominions beyond the Seas, King, Emperor of India, do hereby declare My irrevocable determination to renounce the Throne for Myself and for My descendants, and My desire that effect should be given to this Instrument of Abdication immediately.'

He wrote of the scene later. He was sitting at his desk in the drawing room at Fort Belvedere while around him stood his three brothers, Albert, Duke of York, Henry, Duke of Gloucester, and George, Duke of Kent. 'It was all quite informal. When I had signed the last document. I yielded the chair to my brothers, who in turn appended their signatures as witnesses in their order of precedence. The occasion moved me. Like a swimmer surfacing from a great depth, I left the room and stepped outside, inhaling the fresh morning air.'

Opposite: The Duchess of York hadn't discovered corgis when this picture was taken in 1923 at Glamis Castle. It was ten years later that her children saw a puppy belonging to friends. The Duchess bought one, which they called Dookie, and the Pembroke Corgi has now become a permanent fixture at Buckingham Palace. House dogs, however, were the Duchess's innovation, for Queen Mary didn't like them, and only gun dogs were allowed at Sandringham and Balmoral. The dog pictured here was a favourite from the Duchess's youth. The Bowes-Lyons had always had at least one of this breed of black field spaniels. George V was keen on these dogs and was responsible for the renewed popularity of the much larger Clumber spaniel.

Page 22: This formal portrait was taken in 1926 after the birth of Princess Elizabeth. Duff Cooper, created Lord Norwich in 1952, wrote to his wife Diana of the time he saw them at a play. 'They are such a sweet little couple and so fond of one another. They reminded me of us sitting together in the box having private jokes, and in the interval when we were all sitting in the room behind the box they slipped out, and I found them standing together in a dark corner of the passage talking happily as we might. She affects no shadows of airs or graces.' 1926 was also the year that the Duke of York played at Wimbledon. He partnered his friend Louis Greig in the doubles.

The Duchess of York spent the summer which followed her wedding on the traditional royal family holiday at Balmoral. It is September and she and her husband are pictured next to Queen Mary and the Duke's younger brother Prince George. The latter, who was the same age as David Bowes-Lyon and had been at school with him, was more of a high-liver than his elder brothers. However, he did share with his mother a love of collecting antique furniture, books and paintings. In 1934, shortly before marrying Princess Marina of Greece, he was created Duke of Kent. His children are Prince Edward the current Duke of Kent, Princess Alexandra, and Prince Michael of Kent. Prince George died in a flying accident in Scotland in 1942. It is worth noting that members of the royal family continually change their names as they progress in status. In his lifetime, King George VI was Prince Albert until 1920, and then from 1920 to his accession, as his father put it: 'that fine old title of Duke of York which I bore for more than nine years and is the oldest Dukedom in the country.' This subject once prompted one of Queen Mary's rare jokes. Someone mentioned a lady of fashion whose name had changed as she exchanged husbands no less than seven times. 'Well I have had to change mine quite a lot: Princess May, Duchess of York, Duchess of Cornwall, Princess of Wales, Queen. But whereas mine have been by accident, hers have been by enterprise.'

Norman Parkinson once said that the Princess of Wales is the best member of the royal family to photograph 'in the street'. I maintain the same of Queen Elizabeth. She seems to have the ability to smile at several hundred people at once whilst giving the impression that she is acknowledging each personally. She once told Eleanor Roosevelt that the secret is to pick out an individual in a knot and smile pointedly, and to concentrate on faces in several rows. She is here accompanying my great grandmother to the opening of the British Empire Exhibition by the King at Wembley on 23rd April 1924. That exhibition proved so popular that after it had been closed on 1st November by the Prince of Wales, there was popular demand to reinstate it. On 10th May 1925 the Duke of York, who had taken over from his brother as president of the exhibition, officially reopened it. This was one of his first important public addresses and his stammer had not improved. What was worse was that his father, the King, was in the audience. George V was pleasantly surprised afterwards. He noticed the 'rather long pauses', but put in that 'Bertie got through his speech all right'. Other commentators called it 'agonizing'. It made the Duchess determined that a cure should be found for her husband's speech impediment.

Opposite: The Duke of York went to Hyde Park in 1924 to inspect the Special Constables. In this picture the Duchess of York is talking to Lord Claude Hamilton. Lord Hamilton, who was born in 1843, was the son of the 1st Duke of Abercorn. His mother was Lady Louisa Russell, daughter of the Duke of Bedford. He was a member of parliament for Londonderry, Kings Lynn, and then Liverpool from 1865 to 1888, and in 1887 became an aide-de-camp to Queen Victoria. He married Carolina Chandos-Pole in 1878. He then re-entered parliament as member for South Kensington from 1910 to 1918. In 1893 he became Chairman of the Great Eastern Railway. He died in 1925. He was the great uncle of the Duchess's bridesmaid Lady Katherine Hamilton.

This is one of the first examples of spur-of-the-moment royal photojournalism, during a visit by the Duke and Duchess to Stirling. A man with a basket of flowers leapt forward hoping to present one to the Duchess, but the long arm of the law intervened. The Duchess seems to have been amused. Scotland has always been a special place for her. On a later trip to South Africa a Boer farmer complained that 'we still feel sometimes that we can't forgive the English for conquering us'. – 'I understand perfectly, we feel very much the same in Scotland', came the reply. She has many connections with her homeland. Her favourite residence these days is the Castle of Mey on the north coast, and she is Colonel-in-Chief of the Black Watch. She counts Robert the Bruce as one of her ancestors. Although her childhood at Glamis Castle was largely informal, certainly compared with court life at Buckingham Palace, Lord Strathmore still kept up the tradition of pipers marching around the table after supper. In 1937 she became the first Scottish Queen for some centuries to visit Edinburgh. 'You're a bonnie lass. I wish I'd courted you myself', commented one spirited old Scotsman.

The Duchess gazes admiringly at her daughter in a touching study of mother and child by Speaight. Lady Asquith noted the young Princess's 'large dark-lashed blue eyes' and 'tiny ears set close to a well-shaped head'. Lady Airlie remembered the christening service well: 'She was a lovely baby although she cried so much all through the ceremony that immediately after it her old-fashioned nurse dosed her well from a bottle of dill-water – to the surprise of the modern young mothers present, and the amusement of her uncle, the Prince of Wales.' The Prince of Wales adored his first niece, and was a constant visitor at the nursery at 145 Piccadilly. Apart from her mother and father, the only people to rival the Prince's affection were the King and Queen.

Opposite: Elizabeth Alexandra Mary, hailed as 'The Empire's Little Princess' by the press was born on 26th April 1926. Alexandra was after her great grandmother who had died the year before, and Mary her grandmother. The name Elizabeth had no direct royal connection, but the Duke of York pointed out to the King that it was a good choice 'and there had been no-one of that name in your family for a long time'. On 29th May Cosmo Lang, the Archbishop of York, christened her in the private chapel at Buckingham Palace. 'Poor baby cried', observed Queen Mary after the service. She and the King sponsored the Princess, while the other godparents were the Duke of York's sister Princess Mary, who had always been a close friend of the Duchess, Lady Elphinstone who was the Duchess's sister Mary, and Prince Arthur, Duke of Connaught, Queen Victoria's third son, who died in 1942.

Opposite: This is one of the brightest press pictures of the Duchess of its age. It is easy to see why she was called the Smiling Duchess. *The Times* later noted that the Duchess of York 'lays a foundation stone as though she had just discovered a new and delightful way of spending an afternoon'. She had bought this animal for her daughter on a visit to East Ham, London, in 1926. This was brave indeed as the slump which followed the General Strike hit the East End hard, and popular feeling was wavering on the subject of royalty. There is no doubt that the bear was gratefully received in the royal nursery. The Duchess was to miss Princess Elizabeth dreadfully during the Yorks' forthcoming royal tour. As she wrote to Queen Mary: 'I feel very much leaving. The baby was so sweet playing with the buttons on Bertie's uniform that it quite broke me up.'

On 22nd February the Duke and Duchess arrived at Auckland in New Zealand, and the rain poured down. *HMS Diomede* officially escorted *HMS Renown*, the Yorks' ship, into the harbour, though there was the usual flotilla of small craft trying to catch a glimpse of the royal visitors. As they stepped ashore from the barge there were cheers from the crowd which had assembled around the Admiralty Wharf. The Governor-General Sir Charles Fergusson greeted them more formally. The Prime Minister J G Coates was also there with his cabinet. The Duke then inspected the naval guard of honour before hearing a welcoming address from the Chairman of the Harbour Board. In this picture taken at the ceremony the Duchess is wearing a delphinium blue georgette dress with matching hat.

One correspondent noted of the Yorks' first day in Auckland that 'every man, woman, and child at this particular point seemed to be an amateur photographer, and several hundred "snaps" must have been taken of the Duke and Duchess'. Several thousand would be today's figure, and of a quality unimaginable in 1927. This picture of the Duchess of York in New Zealand has deteriorated badly over the lasty sixty-odd years, but is a good example of early use of a telephoto lens. The Yorks were mobbed by crowds wherever they went in New Zealand, and occasionally had trouble regaining the safety of their car, even on 'quiet' drives to points of interest.

This is one of the earliest pictures of the Duchess fishing, which from an early age was her antidote to shooting, which she never enjoyed despite her husband's aptitude for it, but luckily both were freely available at Glamis Castle. New Zealand boasts some of the most sporting trout in the world, and she managed to take some time off during the world tour of 1927 to go to Lake Taupo, the Torgariro River and to Tokaanu where she caught the eight-pound trout in this photograph. In one day sea-fishing at the Bay of Islands twenty schnapper were landed of which she caught seventeen. She had wisely brought a rod and line with her which her ghillie carries, and there is the much-worn but still distinctive reel by Hardy of Alnwick. She doesn't mind about wet clothes when it comes to sport. Note the sartorial touch of the ghillie's bow-tie.

Opposite: The Duke and Duchess, dressed appropriately, reviewed Boy Scouts and Girl Guides in Adelaide on 30th April 1927 as part of the world tour. This is a rare picture of the Duchess wearing a uniform, which she does not like doing. However, the Guides had always been a part of her life at Glamis, where she had been District Commissioner. The Duke was keen on youth movements as well. Much in the manner that his grandson Prince Charles began the Prince of Wales's Trust, he put his name to the Duke of York's Camp. For the first one, in the summer of 1921, a hundred public schools and a hundred industrial firms sent two boys each to a disused aerodrome near Hythe in Kent. The boys were the Duke's guests. They were there as equals, and the experiment was a success. There were to be seventeen more camps of this sort before the Second World War. As the Duke had said in a speech in New Zealand only a few days before: 'Take care of the children and the country will take care of itself.'

The Duke and Duchess arrived in Australia on 26th March, and went to Sydney, where the Duchess made her only speech of the tour at the University. They were in Melbourne for Anzac Day, which she attended dressed in black, perhaps thinking also of the recent death of her friend and bridesmaid the Hon. Diamond Abercrombie, sister of Major Alexander Hardinge, who was later private secretary to both King Edward VIII and King George VI. There was also a state ball in Melbourne, where she danced with one of the ex-wounded soldiers from Glamis Castle. For the opening of parliament itself, pictured here, 50,000 people were cheering outside as the Duke was handed a golden key to open the door. The Australian National Anthem was sung, led by Dame Nellie Melba, and the Duke gave perhaps his first spontaneous speech. He had to live up to his brother, the Prince of Wales's, immensely successful tour of 1920. By the end of his trip, the Australian press reaction was favourable.

Looking fit and tanned the Duke and Duchess arrived in
Malta in June 1927 on the last leg of their arduous
world tour. *HMS Renown*, which had a crew of 1,300,
moored next to *HMS Warspite*, flagship of Admiral Sir
Roger Keyes, Commander-in-Chief of the Mediterranean
Fleet. They had a picnic with Lord Louis Mountbatten,
who was stationed out there with the Royal Navy, and
that evening the Duke, Lord Mountbatten and Sir
Roger played for the Royal Navy in four chukkers of
polo against the Army on the Marsa Ground. The Navy
won four-one. In the evening there was a display in the
Grand Harbour. Lord Mountbatten moved his yacht
between *Warspite* and *Renown* and the Yorks went aboard
to watch. Searchlights played across the night sky and
fireworks flashed and boomed. There was a procession
of elaborately decorated and lighted small craft,
containing knife-brandishing Turkish corsairs, or Maori
canoes paddled by walnut-stained bluejacket warriors.
The boats of *HMS Cyclops* became a red dragon which
moved over the face of the dark waters behind a figure
of St George with sword and silver armour gleaming.
After Malta they went on to arrive in Gibraltar on 25th
June where the garrison band played the hymn, Now
thank we all our God, as they steamed in, causing
irreverent laughter aboard the ship. Two days later they
were met at Portsmouth by the Duke's three brothers.
They all took the royal train to Victoria Station where
King George and Queen Mary were waiting for them.
The last letter the Duke had received from his father
contained the grave instructions: 'When you kiss Mama
take yr. hat off.'

Elizabeth 1927 Albert

The Duke and Duchess returned home to great acclaim and to Princess Elizabeth. They had received letters about her progress, her first teeth for example, and photographs with Queen Mary, but it was to be a joyful reunion. On 28th June 1927 they greeted the crowds from the balcony of their home at 145 Piccadilly. Photography in the 1920s was not a simple click. This picture would have been taken on a 5×4 inch camera, using cut or plate film. The lens would have probably been 5 inches, and the aperture f4.5. The shutter would have been a fabric blind, opened with a string loop. To set up a telephoto shot, which could only take place in extremely strong light, the photographer would first focus on a ground glass screen. However, everything came together, and this picture is a triumph of the technology of its era.

1928, when this portrait was taken, was a quiet year compared with the excitement of the world tour. There was the Costermongers' Carnival at Finsbury Town Hall in the new year, where the Duke and Duchess danced with pearly kings and queens. The Duchess also went to the Ideal Home Exhibition at Olympia and to a hospital for disabled children in Surrey. In November the King's cold developed into bronchitis and septicaemia. A Council of State was appointed to take over his duties, and this consisted of the Prince of Wales, Queen Mary, the Prime Minister, the Archbishop of Canterbury, the Lord Chancellor and the Duke of York. It was the Duke's first real training for the crown he was later to wear.

Opposite: From being something of an unknown, the young Duchess of York quickly became a leader of fashion. This is a typical study from the late 1920s, involving a technique known as vignetting, which was popular at that time. Note also the extremely shallow depth of field. Everything beyond the chin is out of focus, which serves to highlight the lace hanging down. It was also from around this time that the Duchess adopted the use of a slightly inclined head for official portraits. She was not trying to emphasize a 'best side' in the style of a Hollywood film star, it simply made her look more approachable and less stiffly regal.

Princess Margaret Rose of York was born on 21st August 1930. Princess Elizabeth had been born at 17 Bruton Street, and the Duchess wanted to have her second child at Glamis Castle. This was the first birth in Scotland of a child so close to the throne, since King Charles I was born in Dunfermline in 1600. There was a storm that night, and when the rain had died down the next morning a beacon was lit on nearby Hunter's Hill. A most extraordinary and embarrassing custom, dating back to the 17th century, whereby the Home Secretary of the day was required to be present at the birth of any child close to the throne, was carried out for the last time. Joseph Clynes, upon whom this onerous task fell and who was staying with Lady Airlie for the duration, had been a mill-worker from Oldham and had joined the Labour Party through the Lancashire Gasworkers Union. He was appalled at the practice and was instrumental in ending it. The girl was nearly christened Ann, but this was vetoed. In the end Margaret Rose was chosen, though Princess Elizabeth decided to call her Bud, since she wasn't really a full-grown Rose.

Marcus Adams, and his inspired touch with children, broke the mould of royal photography after the birth of the Yorks' first child in 1926. Until Lord Snowdon arrived on the scene there was only ever one accepted royal photographer at a time. Now several have a crack of the whip. This picture was taken in 1931 and generates the warmth, peace and happiness of ideal family life. A royal child would never before have been allowed to hang onto its parents' necks in this way. The Yorks' image as a close family was born with Adams's photography. In the early 1930s, three women of great importance were employed to look after Princess Elizabeth and Princess Margaret Rose of York. They were Clara Knight, who had been the Duchess of York's nurse, Marion Crawford, who was recommended by Lady Rose Bowes-Lyon as the children's first governess, and Margaret Macdonald, an under-nursemaid, who in the tradition of the faithful Highland servant is still the Queen's dresser. They were otherwise known as Allah, Crawfie and Bobo.

Opposite: This is the only picture I have chosen of King George V, seated here outside the children's cottage of *Y Bthwyn Bach* in the grounds of Royal Lodge on 4th May 1933. He was a notable stickler for formality, but allowed it to slip for his daughter-in-law, who once wrote of him: 'In all the twelve years of having me as a daughter-in-law he never spoke one unkind or abrupt word to me, and was always ready to listen and give advice on one's own silly little affairs. He was so kind and so *dependable*. And when he was in the mood, he could be deliciously funny too!' Also in the picture are the Princesses Margaret and Elizabeth beside him, and Queen Mary beside the Duchess of York.

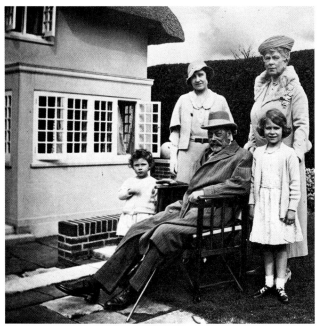

The Duchess of York's parents celebrated their golden wedding anniversary in 1931, a year since Princess Margaret's birth. Here the Duke, Duchess and Princess Elizabeth walk in front of Glamis Castle with the six-year-old the Hon. Margaret Elphinstone. She was the daughter of the Duchess's sister, Lady Mary, who married Sidney, 16th Lord Elphinstone. As head of a Scottish family with origins almost as distinguished and ancient as the Lyons, he held a number of high-ranking posts, including Lord High Commissioner to the General Assembly for the Church of Scotland, Captain of the Queen's Bodyguard for Scotland (Royal Company of Archers), Clerk Register of Scotland and Keeper of the Signet, and Chancellor of the Order of the Thistle. In 1950 Margaret married Denys Rhodes, and their eldest son Simon was page of honour to the Queen from 1971 to 1973.

Opposite above: In 1935 King George V celebrated twenty-five years on the throne. A jubilee service was held at St Paul's Cathedral. This picture was taken as the royal family left the Cathedral, and I find it particularly touching to see the way that Princess Elizabeth is bending down, presumably to get a better view of her grandparents between the legs of the guards. From left to right are: The Duke of York, the Archbishop of Canterbury Cosmo Lang, the Duke of Kent, the Duchess of York, and Princess Marina of Kent.

Opposite below: The Duchess was always on hand to support her husband's work. Here she meets the famous cricketer Jack Hobbs and his wife at the Civil Service Stores' Playing Fields Flag Depot in April 1934. Jack Hobbs, who is widely held to be the best English cricketer ever, was about to play for Surrey for his last season in 1934. In a remarkable career he holds the record for the highest aggregate of runs – over 61,000 – and the greatest number of centuries – 197. His score of 316 not out is the highest made at Lord's. As a national hero he was an ideal figure to help the Yorks endorse the Playing Fields Association. Other societies which the Yorks sponsored included Dr Barnado's Homes, the Gordon Boys' Home and the Fresh Air Fund. This list reflects a regard for health and fitness, and technical efficiency.

This picture shows the Duke of York's ideal. He liked to think of his family as 'us four' and Royal Lodge at Windsor, where this was taken in June 1936, was the family's peaceful weekend retreat. Three-and-a-half year-old Dookie the corgi, whose kennel name was Golden Eagle, is lying in front, facing away from the camera, and eighteen-month-old Jane, registered as Lady Jane, who had a darker mask than Dookie, is out of the picture. The Duchess also had the inevitable Bowes-Lyon black field spaniel, called Ben, which is not pictured here. She is holding her Tibetan terrier, Choo Choo, so-called because when he first came to the family as a puppy he made noises exactly like a train. Later he became known as the Hairy Monster and the Animated Dish Cloth. He wasn't as friendly as the collection of corgis which Queen Elizabeth and her daughters were beginning to amass, and preferred to lie around the palace like a hearth rug. The four yellow labradors pictured here are the Duke's gundogs, Mimsy and her dog and bitch pups Stiffy and Scrummy, and the Duchess's bitch Judy. 1936 was, of course, the year of the three kings. By June, King Edward VIII was half way through his short reign. The Duchess is wearing black in mourning for her father-in-law. Official court mourning finished on 21st July.

In August 1936 the Duke and Duchess visited the Glamis colliery in County Durham, and even the ladies' protective clothes bears out a sense of fashion. The Duke was president of the Industrial Welfare Society from 1919 to 1935, which were arguably the most difficult years for British industry this century. Because of his association with this society the press dubbed him the Industrial Prince.

This picture, from 1936, is a good example of clever use of a telephoto lens. The photographer has managed to keep all the subjects in a plane and thus in focus. The daisies have come out well and are a pretty touch, and Princess Margaret is fidgeting to add to the informality. The other people in the picture are members of the Royal Company of Archers, the Scottish equivalent of the Gentlemen at Arms. It is the sovereign's personal bodyguard while in residence at the Palace of

Holyroodhouse. Based at Archer's Hall in Edinburgh and formally established by royal charter in 1704, it is largely made up of Scottish peers who have also been military officers. These days their numbers include Lord Home of the Hirsel and the Duke of Buccleuch. It is commanded by a captain general, who at the moment is the 13th Earl of Stair, who is married to Davina, the daughter of David Bowes-Lyon. 1936 was a busy year for the Yorks quite apart from any constitutional consideration. The Duchess convalesced in Eastbourne after her illness at the time of George V's death. The family spent Easter and Princess Elizabeth's tenth birthday at Royal Lodge with Queen Mary, and later the five of them went to Southampton to see the brand new liner *Queen Mary*. The Hon. Jean Elphinstone, the Duchess's niece, married John Wills in July, and then there was a tour of the north east of England before travelling to Glamis and Birkhall.

1937-1939
QUEEN AND EMPRESS

'I COMMEND to you his brother, summoned so unexpected and in circumstances so painful, to take his place', said Queen Mary in a moving appeal to the nation. 'With him I commend my dear daughter-in-law who will be his Queen. May she receive the same unfailing affection and trust which you have given me for six-and-twenty years.'

Queen Elizabeth's immediate job was to transfer what she had managed to create at 145 Piccadilly to Buckingham Palace, in order to provide some stability after her family's sudden change of role. As the new King said to Lady Airlie early in 1937, 'Elizabeth could make a home anywhere'. One of her first moves was to cut a swathe through the protocol within which the Palace had been constricted. She was not cutting corners in the way that Edward VIII had insisted on seeing all ambassadors at once instead of individually, she was simply making a more pleasant working atmosphere. Buckingham Palace was more complicated than the house in Piccadilly. It was part home, part offices, part museum, but mostly a tangible example of the monarchy's position as figurehead. None of these attributes could be allowed to drop. The Palace had to be kept on duty at all hours of the day and night. Queen Mary had moved her furniture out five months before, but even so the King and Queen spent the first few weeks in the state apartments for visiting dignitaries, the Belgian suite, on the ground floor, while the children remained at Piccadilly. Soon, Queen Elizabeth's personal touches made it more like home. Not only with the decoration and furniture, but the appointment of a new Assistant Master of the Household in Ririd Myddleton, who had been at Eton with David Bowes-Lyon. By the coronation, the new royal family were firmly ensconced.

The Duke of Norfolk, as Earl Marshal, was in charge of the administration of the coronation. 7,700 invitations were sent out, and arrangements were made for the event to be filmed for newsreels. Queen Elizabeth's dress was made by Handley Seymour with a square décolleté after Van Dyck's portraits. It had originally been intended for her to wear as Duchess of York, but needed only a little adaptation to make it into the gown of a Queen. White and gold emblems of Great Britain and the Empire were embroidered onto it by the Royal School of Needlework. The six maids of honours' dresses were made by Norman Hartnell, who had recently been noticed for his designs for the Duchess of Gloucester's bridesmaids. Cecil Mann, the crown jeweller, designed a new crown for the Queen, and on 12th May 1937 they at last made the jolting ride in the lavish, but uncomfortable Golden State Coach to Westminster Abbey, where the Archbishop of Canterbury, Dr Cosmo Lang, solemnized King George VI's accession. Queen Mary came too, to emphasize the solidarity of the royal family, although it was a break with tradition that the dowager Queen should attend a coronation. As she wrote afterwards, 'Bertie and E did it all beautifully'.

Throughout the rest of 1937 and 1938, the King came to grips with his new job. He was concerned that he was painfully unprepared for it, for King George V, despite his prophetic assertion about his eldest son that 'That boy will ruin himself in a year', had never let the Duke of York look at a state paper. George VI's first year was marked by incessant telephone calls from his brother in France offering advice about how to run the country. Eventually he had to put a stop to them. The Duke of Windsor, as he was now styled, married Wallis Simpson at the Chateau de Candé on 3rd June 1937. They received a well-wishing telegram from 'Bertie and Elizabeth' and also the bad news that a cabinet decision of May 1937 had denied Wallis the honour of putting Her Royal Highness before her name, and that she would have to make do with Her Grace.

On 26th October 1937 the King opened parliament for the first time in his reign. Huge crowds lined the route of the Golden State Coach from Buckingham Palace to Westminster. This was the first full state procession from the Palace since 1933. The King called in his speech therapist Lionel Logue for help with the ordeal. He was worried that in the sitting position on the throne from which he would have to make his speech his specially developed breathing pattern would be broken, and his stammer would return with a vengeance. After several rehearsals Logue was able to allay his fears and despite a few pauses, he delivered the text successfully.

In 1938 the King and Queen made a state visit to France as guests of President Lebrun. Only a few weeks before the Countess Strathmore, Queen Elizabeth's mother, had died aged 76. However, the new Queen still managed to produce her smile. In the words of Lady Diana Cooper, 'Each night's flourish outdid the last'. She visited the Opera, preceded by two *chandeliers*, footmen each carrying a twenty-branched candelabra, and at the Quai d'Orsay she managed to slip past the tortuous French security to wave from a balcony to the thousands who had gathered to cheer. 'France has a monarchy again!' blazed one of the newspaper headlines.

Norman Hartnell, who had designed the Queen's clothes for Paris, was asked to do the same for the state visit to Canada and the United States. The King felt confident enough in 1939 to make the step of becoming the first reigning British monarch to visit those two countries. Part of the trip was an effort to stave off war, or at least to gain the great American sympathy. In the end Hartnell produced as many as six different costumes for each day. The King and Queen finally set sail on the *Empress of Australia*, reaching Wolfe's Bay, Quebec, on 27th May. They toured the country from coast to coast, a 4,500 mile journey, stopping at Toronto, Halifax and Victoria, and places like Moose Jaw and Medicine Hat. The Governor General, Lord Tweedsmuir, better known as novelist John Buchan, wrote that Queen Elizabeth 'has a perfect genius for the right kind of publicity'. They received acclaim wherever they went. Tweedsmuir went on: 'When I induced their Majesties to come out here, I didn't realize I was pulling the string of such a shower-bath.' In Ottawa he recorded that the Queen made the first royal walkabout: 'At the unveiling of the war memorial, where we had some 10,000 veterans, she asked me if it were possible to get closer to them. We went right down among them. We were simply swallowed up! I shall never forget the faces of the Scotland Yard detectives.' The American press correspondents were equally amazed. 'No American President would ever have dared to do that', one of them said. A

Canadian veteran asked her whether she felt she was Scottish or English. 'Since we reached Quebec,' she replied, 'I've been a Canadian.'

In New York the crowds numbered four million. A clever geneaologist, Sir Anthony Wagner, had worked out that Queen Elizabeth was one of the nearest living relatives to George Washington, which added to her popularity. Eleanor Roosevelt noted that she 'never had a crease in her dress nor a hair out of place. I do not see how it is possible to remain so perfectly in character all the time.' Rose Kennedy, mother of the future president, wrote to Mrs Roosevelt from London about what to expect of the Queen: 'She has a very pleasing voice, a beautiful English complexion, great dignity and charm; is simple in manner, stands and holds herself very erect. We talked about the difficulty of sleeping in London, and she was very much amused that I put wax in my ears.'

The King and Queen arrived back in England on 22nd June to be met by their daughters in the Solent aboard the destroyer *Kempenfelt*. They threw themselves immediately into the duties which awaited them in Britain. A tired Neville Chamberlain had done all he could to stave off war, but it now looked inevitable. The Queen felt she ought to acquaint herself better with world affairs, so in the summer of 1939 read Hitler's *Mein Kampf*. She sent a copy to the Foreign Secretary Lord Halifax with a note. 'I do not advise you to read it through, or you might go mad, and that would be a great pity. Even a skip through gives one an idea of his mentality ignorance and obvious sincerity.' On 3rd September 1939, Hitler failed to meet the British Government requirement of pulling his troops out of Poland by midnight. War was declared.

The expression on the face of Queen Elizabeth speaks more about the reality of coronation than any of the splendour of the other characters' ceremonial robes. There is usually an eighteen-month gap between accession and coronation. This time it was only five, as Edward VIII's planned date of 12th May 1937 was adhered to for George VI. It was a trying day. The testing of loud-speakers on Constitution Hill had begun at 3am and woken the royal household. The Duke passed the intervening hours with his breathing practice, but was still too nervous to eat breakfast. The Golden State Coach took them from Buckingham Palace at 10am, and they were cheered by people who had stayed up all night to ensure a good position along the route. 'Sirs, I here present to you, King George, your undoubted King', spoke Dr Lang, the Archbishop of Canterbury. As the words 'God Save the King' rang through Westminster Abbey the peers donned their coronets. Then the Queen, supported by the Duchesses of Norfolk, Rutland, Buccleuch and Roxburghe, was given her crown containing the Koh-i-noor diamond by the Archbishop with the words: 'Receive the Crown of Glory, Honour and Joy', and the peeresses put their coronets on. She couldn't bring herself to smile during the service except at one point, when she saw Princess Margaret, who was sitting between Princess Elizabeth and the Princess Royal, drop a chocolate over the rail of the balcony.

Page 48: This is the official picture from the throne room of Buckingham Palace of 'us four', as the Duke's family were seldom to be again after his accession. He placed great value in his 'quartet' but the pressure of royal duties meant that he was to see little of his children during his sixteen-year reign. In the broadcast which announced his abdication, King Edward VIII had said of his brother: 'He has one matchless blessing, enjoyed by so many of you and not bestowed on me – a happy home with his wife and children.' It is a lot to ask one's brother to become King, but George VI later said: 'With my wife and helpmate by my side, I take up the heavy task which lies before me.'

This is a good telephoto shot considering its date. After the coronation the royal family received huge acclaim from the balcony at Buckingham Palace. Princess Elizabeth practises the famous royal wave as her mother, surrounded by ladies-in-waiting, looks on. The King has an expression on his face most ably put into words by his recent conversation with Lord Mountbatten. 'Dickie, this is absolutely terrible. I never wanted this to happen: I'm quite unprepared for it. David has been trained for this all his life. I've never even seen a state paper. I'm only a naval officer, it's the only thing I know about.' Mountbatten's reply was well put: 'This is a very curious coincidence. My father once told me that, when the Duke of Clarence died, your father came to him and said almost the same thing that you have said to me now, and my father answered: "George, you're wrong. There is no more fitting preparation for a King than to have been trained in the Navy."'

Opposite: This is the Garter Ceremony at Windsor Castle in 1937. On 14th December 1936, his birthday, the King conferred on the Queen the Order of the Garter. She wrote to Queen Mary about it: 'He had discovered that Papa gave it to you on his, Papa's, birthday, 3rd June, and the coincidence was so charming that he has now followed suit and given it to me on his birthday.' In July 1937 the King invested his wife further with the Order of the Thistle in St Giles's Cathedral, Edinburgh. As a coronation present he gave her a Thistle badge and star made of South African diamonds. He later joked: 'We have only one Thistle. I wear it one night, the Queen the next.'

In June 1937 the King and Queen made their traditional visit to Ascot. It was amongst the last Royal Ascot weeks as they were never to be again. It didn't take place during the war, and as *The Times* commented in 1946 'Royal Ascot has been restored to the calendar of social events, but, like much in our new peacetime, its grandeur is greatly diminished'. These days it is more of a showbusiness event than an example of majesty. The group in the royal box are from right to left: the Queen, the King, the Duke of Kent, the Duchess of Kent, the Duchess of Gloucester, the Princess Royal, the Duke of Gloucester and the Earl of Harewood.

Opposite above: On 11th November 1937, Armistice Day, the King attended the Service of Remembrance at the Cenotaph in Whitehall. It was the nineteenth anniversary of the Armistice, and the first hints of Britain's second war with Germany in twenty-five years were beginning to filter through. Here the Queen is leaving the service by the Clive Steps with Sir Samuel Hoare. Sir Samuel, later Viscount Templewood, had been made First Lord of the Admiralty in 1936. He was a staunch supporter of Edward VIII's right to marry Mrs Simpson and remain King, and he admired her himself. 'Very attractive and intelligent,' he judged after a dinner

given by Edward VIII in his honour. However, he also had praise for the new King and Queen during a tour of Wales and Northern Ireland in 1937: 'When the staff and I could scarcely stand at the end of the day they would remain alert, talking, asking, remembering names and faces.' He went on to serve with distinction in the war. He died without an heir in 1959.

Opposite below: On 14th November 1937 the King and Queen attended morning service at the parish church of St Paul's Walden in Hertfordshire. This picture shows them leaving the church after the service with my great uncle, David Bowes-Lyon. The Queen unveiled a stone tablet to commemorate the fact that she was born in the parish and baptized in the church. *The Times* notice added that 'Their Majesties wish the service to be a very quiet one and the congregation will be limited to the usual worshippers resident in the village. Admission to the service will be by ticket only.' Baptized in the church she was, but she was actually born in London, and the birthplace on her birth certificate is wrong because her father had registered it in a hurry, and had been fined for registering it too late. It was the *Sunday Times* which, over forty years later, noticed the discrepancy.

Opposite: On 29th March 1938 the King and Queen inspected the new London County Council flats in Clarissa Street. These were built in the poor area of Shoreditch. Today, because of its convenience for the city, this area is becoming extremely desirable. The King and Queen took more genuine interest in the plight of poverty than Edward VIII had. The latter would visit coal mining communities during the depression and with a look of greatest concern say that something must be done. The King and Queen would take an active interest in the way that organizations in charge of reshaping depressed areas actually worked. Lady Elphinstone, the Queen's sister, once said, 'they were so particularly together; they both leant so much on the other.' Perhaps that was the reason for their success.

Above: On 12th April 1938 the King and Queen visited Aldershot in Hampshire where they watched a demonstration of troops in action as well as infantry and tanks taking part in an attack. The programme also included the inspection of a cookhouse, troops at dinner, quarters for newly-married soldiers, and a school for soldiers' children. In this picture they are watching the loading of a three-inch mortar during their visit to the range near Chobham Ridges. In a speech a year later before war had broken out, the King said: '... this demonstration of the spirit of service which is everywhere present in the nation today, and which shows itself in the determination to make the country ready to meet any emergency whatever the sacrifices or inconveniences entailed. You know that all our preparations are designed not to provoke war but to preserve peace.'

Opposite: On 10th June 1938 there was a Girl Guide rally at Windsor. Here the Queen and her two daughters are standing in the quadrangle. Following their mother's keen interest in the movement both of the Princesses joined. In 1938 Princess Elizabeth was a Guide (Kingfisher Patrol) and Princess Margaret a Brownie (Leprechaun Six). They had joined the year before. When the Queen wasn't sure how to introduce her daughters to new friends the Guides were the solution. Although the Buckingham Palace pack stopped for the war, they set up in Windsor as an evacuee company in 1942. This was one of the few activities the royal children were allowed to involve themselves in during the war years. Their fellow Guides came from a Hammersmith school, which had been evacuated to Windsor, and from the Royal School in Home Park. Princess Elizabeth also supported her father when he took the salute from the Boy Scouts at Windsor. The Princesses were the inspiration for many of the country's children, especially during the war years, just as their parents were for the nation's adults.

On 5th August 1938 the King and the Queen attended the Braemar Games with their daughters. These Highland games have an interesting history. In the eleventh century King Malcolm III of Scotland summoned the clans to meet at the Braes of Mar in order to pick from them the 'hardiest soldiers and fleetest messengers'. Then in 1715 the Earl of Mar raised the standard for the Jacobite rebellion in that great crossroads of the north. It was to end in his defeat at the Battle of Sherriffmuir, but by now Braemar was becoming established as one of the major venues for the gatherings of clans. Queen Victoria began the royal association with these events by visiting the gathering at Invercauld in 1848. Two years later the Braemar Games had become an annual royal event. As she wrote in her journal, 'There were the usual games of putting the stone, throwing the hammer and caber, and racing up the hill of Craig Cheunnich, which was accomplished in less than six minutes and a half; and we were all much pleased to see our ghillie Duncan, who is an active, good-looking young man, win.'

The King, the Queen, Neville Chamberlain with his dry
expression, and the formidable Mrs Chamberlain, pose
for the press on 30th September 1938. The Queen had
launched her namesake, the ship the *Queen Elizabeth*
only three days before on Clydeside in front of a quarter
of a million people, and she and the King had travelled
down by train from Balmoral the night before. It was the
day after Chamberlain's visit to see Hitler in Munich.
That morning he had descended from his 'plane
brandishing the piece of paper which read: 'We regard
the agreement signed last night and the Anglo-German
naval agreement as symbolic of the desire of our two
peoples never to go to war with one another again. We
are resolved that the method of consultation shall be the
method adopted to deal with any other questions that
may concern our two countries.'

On their way to their tour of Canada and the United States on 14th May 1939 the King and Queen posed for photographers during a lifeboat drill aboard the royal liner *Empress of Australia*. The Canadian Prime Minister Mackenzie King had asked the King and Queen to visit his country when he was in London for the coronation. Franklin D Roosevelt also sent a letter of invitation. 'I need not assure you that it would give my wife and me the greatest pleasure to see you, and frankly I think it would be an excellent thing for Anglo-American relations if you could visit the United States.' The voyage was not without its excitements. Queen Elizabeth wrote to Queen Mary about it: 'For three and a half days we only moved a few miles. The fog was so thick that it was like a white cloud around the ship, and the foghorn blew incessantly. Its melancholy blasts were echoed back by the icebergs like the twang of a piece of wire. Incredibly eerie, and really very alarming, knowing that we were surrounded by ice, and unable to see a foot either way. We very nearly hit a berg, the day before yesterday, and the poor captain was nearly demented because some kind cheerful people kept on reminding him that it was about here that the *Titanic* was struck, and *just* about the same date!'

The King and Queen's visit to the United States was a success. The King became the first reigning British monarch to set foot in the country. However the threat of war hung like the Sword of Damocles over the trip. Mrs Roosevelt wrote in her diary of the royal party's departure: 'As the train pulled out someone began singing Auld Lang Syne, and it seemed to me that there was something of our friendship and our sadness and something of the uncertainty of our futures in that song that I could not have said in any other words.' Seated on the porch of the Roosevelt family home at Hyde Park NY on 19th June 1939 are from left to right: Mrs Franklin D Roosevelt, the King, the President's mother Mrs Sarah Roosevelt, the Queen, and President Roosevelt.

Opposite: This is one of Cecil Beaton's finest pictures, at Buckingham Palace in July 1939. The sense of design was of the highest importance in his pictures. He was a favourite royal photographer and was responsible for many of Queen Elizabeth's anniversary portraits. He had that most important talent of making his subject, however famous, powerful or charismatic, pose exactly as he wanted. Queen Elizabeth is wearing one of the dresses with which she had conquered Paris and Canada. They were designed by Norman Hartnell in the style of the Empress Eugenie's crinolines. However, five days before the King and Queen were to leave for France, the Queen's mother, the Countess Strathmore died. The visit was put back three weeks, but there was no possibility that the Queen could continue to wear her dazzling new wardrobe. Luckily the official colours for mourning include white and purple as well as black, and so in the last week all her clothes were remade to the same designs, but in white Valenciennes lace, picked out in silver. Beaton was able to use the colour of her clothes to give this picture an ethereal quality which suits Queen Elizabeth. However, he has expended at least as much attention on the background as the sitter. He had a great sense of scale. After one sitting he asked Queen Elizabeth whether she would like him to retouch any of the lines on her face, 'I would not want it to be thought that I had lived for all these years without having anything to show for it', came the reply – shades of Oliver Cromwell with his warts and all. This set of pictures was not published until after war was declared, and she thought they might be inappropriate considering the nation's new sense of austerity. However, glamour turned out to be exactly what everyone wanted and other photographs in this series were made into Christmas cards sent to all armed forces personnel bearing the message: 'May God bless and protect you, Elizabeth R George RI.'

1939-1945
THE WAR

*'In the darkest hour of man's despair
lies woman's mission.'*
Queen Elizabeth

IN 1935 George V had told his Prime Minister Lloyd George: 'I *will not* have another war! The last war was none of my doing, and if there is another one and we are threatened with being brought into it, I will go to Trafalgar Square and wave a red flag myself sooner than allow this country to be brought in!'

The beginning of the Second World War was marked by a reluctance to fight, but by a surge of nationalist feeling, which the royal family did all they could to instil with confidence. In a broadcast on the wireless to the women of Britain, France and Poland, the Queen said: 'The greater your devotion and courage, the sooner we shall see the happy ordered life for which we long.' At the same time she became Commandant-in-Chief of the Wrens, Waafs and Waacs. She never wore a uniform, for she felt she didn't have the figure for it. Her clothes took on the peculiar stamp by which the world knows her today, of pinks, lilacs and blues. 'Dusty is an apt colour, it doesn't show the dust on bomb sites', she said.

The Queen managed to put over to the public some semblance of normal life. There were art exhibitions and concerts at the heavily sandbagged National Gallery. It all helped to prove that Britain was indomitable. However, in May 1940 Adolf Hitler's army swept through western Europe until he stood, as Napoleon once had, overlooking the English Channel. 335,000 British troops escaped from Dunkirk, and foreign royalty appeared as well. Queen Wilhelmina of Holland arrived in what she had been wearing when picked up by a British destroyer. King Haakon of Norway came to take command of the Norwegian resistance. King Zog of Albania brought his wife Queen Geraldine to London, and their neighbour, the young King Peter of Yugoslavia came with his government, allowing his regent, Prince Paul, to find refuge in Kenya. King Peter found that this was a good opportunity to go to Cambridge. Even King George of the Hellenes came to London briefly from a temporary stay in Egypt. He tried to run his country from Claridges, but soon returned to set up a more formal government-in-exile in Cairo. The King of Denmark and the King of the Belgians remained in their own countries under occupation.

As for the British royal family's security in the event of the capture of London, Colonel J S Coates led the Coates Mission which prepared four safe houses in Scotland, Worcestershire, North Wales and Dorset to receive them. The word 'Cromwell' was the code word for imminent invasion. However, the Queen took up pistol practice, preferring to go down with guns blazing.

Goering's Luftwaffe began to bomb British cities in earnest in September 1940, drawing on experience from the Spanish civil war, and even Buckingham Palace was hit. For the King and Queen it meant an endless saddening round of visits to bomb sites, trying to bring some consolation to people whose houses had been reduced to dust. Lilian Bowes-Lyon, the Queen's first cousin, showing some of the family spirit, headed the Womens' Voluntary Service on the Bow Road in the East End. She fearlessly used her connections to bring relief during the Blitz. The Queen addressed women civil defence workers at the end of 1944: 'I believe strongly that when future generations look back on this terrible war they will recognize as one of its chief features the degree to which women were actively concerned in it. I do not think it is any exaggeration to say that in this country, at any rate, the war could not have been won without their help. That is a thought which gives me pride as a woman.'

Home life was almost as difficult for the royal family as for anybody. Their food was rationed – one egg each per fortnight, for example – and they were issued with clothing coupons. The carpets at Buckingham Palace were noticeably threadbare and the dresses with which the Queen had stunned America came out again and again. The Princesses were confined to Windsor Castle, apart from the odd trip to their dentist in London. Other members of the royal family fared worse. In August 1942 the family was shattered by the death of the Duke of Kent in a Sunderland flying boat accident. His son Prince Michael had been born only a few weeks before.

The war finally turned in the Allies' favour with the surrender of the Axis forces in North Africa in June 1943. The King flew out to review his troops. His journey, after Prince George's death, put a great strain on the Queen. He returned safely, but a new and more sinister phase of the war on the home front was about to begin. The V1 pilotless planes or doodlebugs, began to hum overhead, suddenly cut out, and then make their deadly descent. A V1 destroyed the Guards' Chapel near Buckingham Palace during morning service on the Sunday of the first week of this airborne terror. 120 members of the congregation were killed, including many of the King and Queen's oldest friends. The V1s were eventually replaced by the silent and even more frightening V2s. There was no doubt, though, that by now Germany was on the run.

Just as Queen Elizabeth was feeling more confident of victory her father, Lord Strathmore, my great grandfather, died at the age of 89, the funeral was at Glamis, and she and the King followed the sad procession of pipers from the Black Watch to the family burial ground. Another blow came with the death of their old friend Franklin D Roosevelt in April 1945. They had just planned to make a trip to the United States to see him.

The crowds gathered in The Mall and around Westminster the day before the signing of peace on 7th May 1945. Eventually a quarter of a million people were standing outside the Palace, chanting 'We want the King! We want the Queen!' There was a burst of euphoria for the whole of that week before the task of picking up the pieces of broken lives began. The austerity was to continue for some years. Millions of refugees milled around Europe, war criminals were trying to escape, and there was considerable work for Queen Elizabeth yet to do.

The words of the King at the end of the war with Japan sum it up most keenly: 'The war is over. You know, I think, that those four words have, for the Queen and myself, the same significance, simple yet immense, that they have for you. Yet there is not one of us who has experienced this terrible war who does not realize that we shall feel its inevitable consequences long after we have all forgotten our rejoicings of today.'

On 27th November 1939, three months after war began, the King, Queen and other members of the royal family went to see a performance of George Black's Black Velvet starring Vic Oliver. This picture is of extremely good quality considering that it was taken in such difficult circumstances. The only light available was that reflected from the stage. From left to right the party in the royal box consists of Princess Marina Duchess of Kent, Prince George Duke of Kent, Princess Alice Duchess of Gloucester, the King, the Queen, and Prince Henry Duke of Gloucester. When the news of the war came through, George VI broadcast to the nation. His speech ended: 'The task will be hard, there may be dark days ahead, and war can no longer be confined to the battlefield, but we can only do the right as we see the right, and reverently commit our cause to God. If one and all we keep resolutely faithful to it ready for whatever sacrifice it may demand, then, with God's help, we shall prevail. May he bless and keep us all.'

Page 66: By 1942, when this picture was taken, there was a prospect of victory, however slim. Britain no longer stood alone now that America was in the war. Nonetheless the King wrote in his diary 'I cannot help feeling depressed at the future outlook.' A few days before the picture was taken the King had received Soviet Foreign Minister Molotov to discuss the arrangements for the Anglo-Soviet Treaty of Alliance. Despite everything being in the balance, the royal family here display the simple, strong, determined unity that inspired the nation throughout the war.

Queen Elizabeth inspects Australian troops on 27th June 1940 at the Victoria League Club, where soldiers and sailors from all parts of the Empire were staying when in London. Over three hundred thousand troops had been evacuated from France earlier that month. This had meant that security for the King and Queen had to be tightened. They were assigned a bullet-proof car, and steel helmets to go with their gas-masks, the Queen also took up small arms practice. Lord Halifax, the Foreign Secretary, used to use the grounds of Buckingham Palace as a shortcut to Whitehall. One morning his constitutional was violently interrupted by gunfire nearby. When he learnt that it was Queen Elizabeth and her ladies-in-waiting popping off at imaginary German paratroopers on the newly erected range he turned round and didn't use that route again.

Opposite: This study by Marcus Adams from April 1940 is sugary by today's standards but was fashionable then. It was designed as a palliative for the masses. That spring marked the end of the phoney war. Hitler invaded Denmark and Norway on 9th April. The evacuation of a million children from cities all over Britain had taken place, and the Queen sent a personal message to each of the families they went to: 'You have earned the gratitude of those to whom you have shown hospitality, and by your readiness to serve you have helped the State in a work of great value.' When asked whether she thought the two Princesses would be safer in Canada the Queen replied, 'The children won't go without me. I won't leave the King. And the King will never leave.'

Hitler's policy of Blitzkrieg on major British cities began in September 1940. This picture was taken on 11th and shows the King and Queen during a tour of bomb damage in South London. Their old home, 145 Piccadilly, sustained a direct hit that month and was completely destroyed, though luckily it was empty. It was an important part of the Queen's war work to console people and offer comfort and encouragement.

She showed real concern, especially with nurses. She went to other areas of the country which had suffered badly, including Plymouth, Bath and Coventry. Winston Churchill penned a note of thanks to the King: 'This war has drawn the throne and the people more closely together than ever before, and Your Majesties are more beloved by all classes and conditions than any of the princes of the past.'

A bomb fell in the grounds of Buckingham Palace on 10th September 1940 shattering windows on the north and west sides. Then on 13th as one policeman pointed out: 'A magnificent piece of bombing, Ma'am, if you'll pardon my saying so', took place. It was magnificent in that all but one of the bombs landed on open ground. The one that caused damage destroyed the chapel and a plumber's workshop, which is what the King, the Queen and Winston Churchill are inspecting here. It is now the site of the Queen's Gallery. At the time of the raid the King and Queen were working in a room overlooking the quadrangle with Alexander Hardinge, brother of Diamond, Queen Elizabeth's bridesmaid. This sudden brutal attack prompted the Queen's famous line: 'I'm glad we've been bombed. It makes me feel I can look the East End in the face.'

Opposite: The Princesses Elizabeth and Margaret spent the war at Windsor. As Princess Margaret said later, 'We packed for the weekend and stayed for five years. We were not allowed to go far from the house in case there were air raids; there had been a pathetic attempt to defend the Castle with trenches and some rather feeble barbed wire. It would not have kept anyone out, but it did keep us in.' In this picture of 8th July 1941 they are having lessons in the garden of Royal Lodge. Princess Elizabeth received additional history lessons from Sir Henry Marten, Vice-Provost of Eton. During the course of the war over two hundred bombs fell on Windsor Great Park. One flattened the two cottages at the entrance to the Royal Lodge. A gatekeeper and his wife died in the explosion.

This picture is from the same set as the last one, but is a much more daring composition. It is more exciting than a fireplace picture, and has a great sense of design. Towards the end of the war Princess Elizabeth joined the Auxiliary Territorial Service as all girls aged sixteen were required to do. She was 2nd lieutenant, No. 230873, and learnt the skills of a motor mechanic and military driver. She wore her ATS uniform on VE day. It is ironic that at the outbreak of World War I Queen Elizabeth had been just fourteen years old, and her future husband a midshipman in the Navy. History repeated itself. In 1939 Princess Elizabeth was also in her early teens, and her future husband was learning to be an officer in the senior service.

London Underground stations were quickly turned over
to bomb shelters and even temporary housing in the
Blitz. Here the King and the Queen visit one on 14th
November 1940, the night that the Luftwaffe destroyed
Coventry. The King would not allow her to witness that
carnage immediately, and went alone to the devastated
city the next day. Coventry has now been rebuilt, and
the only reminder of that fateful night, when forty acres
were flattened, is the ruined shell of the old cathedral. It
stands as an approach to the new cathedral, which was
designed by Sir Basil Spence and consecrated in 1962.
There is a wooden cross made from two charred beams
on the old cathedral's altar bearing the inscription
'Father Forgive'.

Queen Elizabeth felt she had to find some form of relief
for Coventry's citizens. She had helped Lord Woolton to
set up, with American Aid, a fleet of vehicles bringing
meals to badly hit areas. The women-drivers of these
convoys were called the Queen's Messengers. The first
convoy rolled out of the depot to go to Coventry where
they fed 12,000 for three days. Lord Woolton was born
in 1883. He was an able administrator and for that was
made Minister of Food in 1940, and then in 1943
Minister of Reconstruction. He was chairman of the
Conservative Party from 1946 to 1955 and died in 1964.
This picture was taken in the courtyard at Buckingham
Palace in 1941.

Queen Elizabeth and Lady Louis Mountbatten,
Superintendent-in-Chief of the St John Ambulance
Brigade, look at a stall at the Allied Nations Summer
Fair in the gardens of Clarence House, London, on 26th
June 1943. The King had just returned from a tour of
North Africa where he had reviewed victorious troops.
He had travelled from Northolt Airport via Gibraltar
under the name of General Lyon. The subterfuge had
been further enhanced by an investiture at the Palace at
which the King would normally be present. However, he
appointed Queen Elizabeth a Counsellor of State, and
while he was away she became the first woman since
Queen Victoria to preside at this ceremony. Wing
Commander Guy Gibson of the Dam Busters was
present to receive his Victoria Cross. Palace officials
began to mutter, though, when it took four hours to
decorate the 255 officers and men. The Queen insisted
on talking to everybody present.

On VE Day, 8th May 1945, the King, the Queen and the Princesses Elizabeth and Margaret went out onto the balcony at Buckingham Palace eight times, though it was uncertain how safe the balcony was. Note that the windows are boarded up. On one occasion they were accompanied by Winston Churchill. Their first appearance was immediately after the signing of the Act of Surrender by the Germans at Rheims. They then went out at 4.15 and 5.30 with Churchill. In response to the continuing enthusiasm of the vast crowds they went out for the last time at 12.30am. During that afternoon the two Princesses had been allowed to slip out to join the celebrations among the throng outside the Palace gates.

Opposite: Although the Princesses spent most of the war at Windsor this picture was taken at Buckingham Palace in 1942. Allied morale was at a low ebb at the time as both Singapore and the garrison at Tobruk capitulated to Axis forces the Queen's nephew John, was killed at Halfaya Pass, and another nephew was taken prisoner. Her old home St Paul's Walden Bury was turned into a hospital, and her greatest friend, her brother David, was sent away to New York to become head of the Political Warfare mission. This picture was intended to show that the royal family was keeping the home fires burning, the King in uniform, and the Queen and Princesses in respectably dowdy grey. The lighting in the picture is a bit austere as well. I remember how flexes used to feed lamps and how we made no attempt to tidy or hide them, but with a minimum of forethought they need not have been so obvious here.

1946-1952
YEARS OF AUSTERITY

'A flash of colour on the hard road we travel.'
Winston Churchill

WITH the end of the war with Japan, peace broke out on 15th August 1945, but the austerity was to continue as Europe groped around for agriculture and its manufacturing industries. However, the King and Queen were able to take a long-awaited holiday with their family at Balmoral that summer, surrounded by friends, more a clan than a royal house. The King spent his days teaching his eldest daughter the rudiments of stalking, while the Queen organized picnics on the estate.

During the period directly after the war there were victory garden parties, a new generation of diplomats to forge links with, and, in June 1946, a grand Victory Parade through London watched by a crowd of an estimated eleven million people, a quarter of Britain's population. The King and Queen took the salute in The Mall. A Labour Government won the general election, and the King acquainted himself with his first new set of politicians for eight years. The preparations for the first post-war tour began. The King, Queen and Princesses Elizabeth and Margaret left for South Africa in January 1947, during one of Britain's bitterest winters, with electricity rationed as trains carrying coal were unable to reach the power stations through snowdrifts. The tour, which included parts of Rhodesia, was a gruelling 10,000 mile journey in an ivory and gold train. Queen Elizabeth insisted that they wave at the remotest farmsteads along the way. It took two months, during which the King lost nearly a stone, and ended with Princess Elizabeth's 21st birthday celebrations at Government House in Cape Town.

Only a few weeks after the royal family's return to England the Princess's engagement to Lieutenant Philip Mountbatten RN was announced. He had been born Prince Philip of Greece on 19th June 1921 in Corfu. His surname, had he ever needed one, would have been Schleswig-Hölstein-Sonderburg-Glücksburg. He was really a member of the royal house of Denmark, once hailed as the greatest exporting royal family of the century. His early life was spent with a procession of relations as his family was forced into exile, and he stayed for a while at Kensington Palace. He shares Queen Victoria as a common ancestor with the Queen. The people he ended up with more and more though were the Mountbattens, until Lord Louis Mountbatten had became something of a guardian to him, and as great an influence as the founder of his school, Gordonstoun, Kurt Hahn. Because of Prince Philip's links with the Greek royal family and in turn their relationship to the ex-Kaiser of Germany, it was inconceivable to allow the engagement to go ahead until he had renounced any claim to the Greek throne. When he had done that, and become Anglican from Greek Orthodox, he chose the surname Mountbatten for the purposes of the engagement announcement. Although he had only been allowed a limited commission in the Navy due to his nationality, he won the King's Dirk at Dartmouth, and was mentioned in despatches in the war after the British landing on Crete. The couple were married on 20th November 1947, and Prince Philip was given the titles Duke of Edinburgh, Earl of Meirioneth and Baron Greenwich, to represent Scotland, Wales and England. He was also accorded the style His Royal Highness.

On 26th April 1948 the King and Queen celebrated twenty-five years of marriage. They both spoke on the wireless, and the Queen's speech included the words: 'There must be many who feel as we do that the sanctities of married life are in some way the highest form of human fellowship, affording a rock-like foundation on which all the best in the life of the nation is built. Looking back over the last twenty-five years, and to my childhood, I realize more and more that wonderful sense of security and happiness which comes from a loved home.'

On 23rd November 1948 the following announcement was made by Buckingham Palace. 'His Majesty has agreed to cancel all public engagements over a period of some months. This decision involves the indefinite postponement of the visit to Australia and New Zealand which the King and Queen had undertaken to pay, with Princess Margaret, during the first half of next year. Their Majesties wish to express to the people of Australia and New Zealand their profound regret and bitter disappointment.'

King George began to suffer cramp during that summer. He had obstructions in his major arteries, and nearly had to have his legs amputated. Prince Charles was born in November as the King lay ill. He still needed an operation, performed on 12th March the next year. He was put under the care of Professor Learmouth, and while recovering he produced a sword from under his pillow and knighted his surgeon on the spot. 'You used a knife on me; now I'm going to use one on you.'

Between 1949 and 1951, when Princess Elizabeth also had to start supporting her father as his health began to fail, she and Prince Philip enjoyed their happiest days as a nearly normal couple stationed in Malta with the Navy. The King's condition improved steadily during 1950, though pressures on him that year included the devaluation of the pound against the dollar by thirty per cent, Clement Attlee's Labour government's policy of nationalization, and then the beginning of the Korean War on 25th June. However, it was mooted that the King and Queen should once again think about a tour of Australia and New Zealand. Princess Elizabeth, who gave birth to Princess Anne that year, and Prince Philip planned a tour of Canada and the United States which finally took place in 1951, though they waited for the King to have a lung operation. They returned in November in order to celebrate Christmas at Sandringham. It should have been especially happy for Queen Elizabeth, but she had learnt in mid September that the King had lung cancer. It was to be his last Christmas. Then the Edinburghs were off again, to Australia and New Zealand via East Africa. Just before they left, King George VI's family 'quartet', with the addition of Prince Philip, went to see the musical South Pacific at Drury Lane.

While the Princess was staying at Treetops in Kenya the news came to her via Reuters, a journalist from the *East African Standard*, Prince Philip's private secretary Commander Michael Parker, and then the Duke of Edinburgh himself, of the King's peaceful death on the night of 5th February 1952. Back at Sandringham, Queen Elizabeth had become Queen Mother, and more poignantly, a widow at the age of fifty-one.

These family groups and the one on page 80 were taken at Royal Lodge on 8th July 1946. Their theatricality was fashionable at the time, though in this sort of photography there is a fine line between the relaxed and the skittish. Two of the pictures show the royal family with Princess Elizabeth's Tibetan terrier Chin. Chin was the grandson of Choo Choo, Queen Elizabeth's dog, and the last of that breed owned by a member of the royal family. There is also in the set a fine example of hand-tinting! The artist has skipped the horse, the gravel and parts of the trees. The result is not only odd colouring, but a strange fuzziness. A love of riding has become something of a trademark for the royal family. However, Princess Elizabeth had a serious riding accident in the autumn of 1945 and spent several days in bed. Luckily this turned out to be a good opportunity for the fifteen-year-old Princess Margaret to take on some of her duties. The King recognized in his younger daughter the keenness that he had felt to take a part in public life during his father's last years, and allowed her to make a speech in place of her sister. 'Now that the long years of war are over and the victory is won we must look forward with glad determination and courage to the tasks which lie ahead,' she said. What comes over most strongly from this set is a sense of rationing, both material and emotional. As the King said of his daughters in 1945, 'Poor darlings, they have never had any fun yet.'

Opposite: Beaton at his flamboyant and stylish best, with his use of grand theatrical backdrops. He had the knack of getting proportions just right. The picture was taken at Buckingham Palace in 1948. On 26th April that year the King and Queen celebrated their silver wedding anniversary. They drove with Princess Margaret in the sunshine on a tour of London. Six Windsor greys drew the State Landau as crowds lined their route to a thanksgiving service at St Paul's Cathedral. Afterwards they gave a lunch at Buckingham Palace with guests from many of the royal families of Europe. Winston Churchill called the day 'a flash of colour on the hard road we travel'.

On 27th July 1949 the Queen made a surprise visit to the garden of Mr and Mrs A E Cook of Warner Place, Bethnal Green. They had only a few hours warning that she was making a lightning tour of prize-winning gardens in a competition sponsored by the London Garden Society. In this picture the Queen is chatting to Mrs Cook in her back garden. Queen Elizabeth's love of gardening had been instilled from an early age by her mother, my great grandmother, the Countess Strathmore. Her spare time was taken up to some extent with the health and beauty of the many royal gardens. She and the King were personally responsible for the existence of Royal Lodge's lawns and borders.

I like this colour picture of the Epsom Derby on the first Wednesday in June, 1947, because it is particularly notable for the fashion element. Post-war austerity had brought a demand for sensible clothing. Gone are the morning coats, top hats and wonderful outfits that would have been seen in 1939, and 1989 for that matter! The great race was won that year by G Bridgland on *Pearl Diver*, owned by the Baron de Waldner, at 40–1. The race was named after the twelfth Earl of Derby in the eighteenth century during one of his better parties. The other great race at Epsom is the Oaks, named after the Earl's house nearby. As Lord Rosebery said, 'A roystering party at a country house founded two races, and named them gratefully after their host and his house, the Derby and the Oaks. Seldom has a carouse had a more permanent effect.'

Opposite: Rumours began fly about the Princess's engagement to a certain Lieutenant Philip Mountbatten. These were denied, but the Princess didn't help matters by keeping his picture on her mantelpiece. When it was pointed out to her that this might be indiscreet, she substituted a photograph of her future husband sporting a large seaworthy beard: as a disguise. On 10th July 1947 the following announcement was made by Buckingham Palace: 'It is with the greatest pleasure that the King and Queen announce the betrothal of their dearly beloved daughter The Princess Elizabeth to Lieutenant Philip Mountbatten, R.N., son of the late Prince Andrew of Greece and Princess Andrew (Princess Alice of Battenberg), to which union the King has gladly given his consent.' In this formal engagement picture the dreaded tungsten film lighting is obvious. It required a lot of setting up, and was used until the 1960s when studio pro flash came in.

The Queen holds her first grandchild, the infant Prince Charles of Edinburgh, after his christening at Buckingham Palace on 15th December 1948. He was born on 14th November. At that time his grandfather was lying ill in another part of the Palace. The crowds which had gathered outside the gates to cheer the child in were asked to be quiet, for both the King's and the Prince's sakes. Luckily the King recovered enough to take part in his grandson's christening. Prince Charles wore the royal christening robe of Honiton lace and white silk which had been made for Queen Victoria's children. He slept peacefully throughout the service. His nurse, sister Helen Rowe, stands just out of the frame of this picture, which was taken in the Music Room.

The King was well enough to attend Prince Charles's third birthday party on 15th November 1951. This was the first picture of him after he had had his left lung removed, following a blockage in one of the bronchial tubes. Other guests at the party included Queen Elizabeth, Queen Mary, and the Duke and Duchess of Gloucester. Princess Elizabeth and Prince Philip had left for a tour of Canada, which had already been postponed due to the King's condition. In this flash photograph, Prince Charles and the one-year-old Princess Anne are sitting with the King and Queen. This picture remains one of the present Queen's favourites. A copy of it is on her desk at Buckingham Palace to this day.

The King died during the night of 5th February 1952.
He had felt well enough to go shooting with local
farmers that day, while the Queen and Princess
Margaret had gone to visit the artist Edward Seago
nearby. King George had enjoyed the strenuous
attention of his grandchildren in the nursery before
supper, and had gone to bed as usual in the ground
floor room which he had been using since his illness.
His valet was unable to wake him the next morning. His
body lay in the chapel at Sandringham for four days, and
then in state in Westminster Hall. This is the sombre
picture of the three Queens, the King's mother, wife
and daughter, at the funeral on 15th February. It has
become one of the most famous images of the century.

Although black and white was the accepted norm for photographs in 1952, the dignity of this picture would certainly have been lost in colour. The columns draped in black are particularly striking. The coffin was drawn by Royal Naval ratings on a gun carriage from Westminster Hall to Paddington Station to be taken to Windsor. The occasion is particularly clear in my own memory, because I was in London with my sister to watch my father commanding one of the detachments accompanying the procession. The coffin is here about to be put aboard the royal train. Veiled in black can be seen Queen Elizabeth, now called the Queen Mother, the Princess Royal, the Queen and Princess Margaret. Behind them stand the Duke of Windsor, the Duke of Kent, the Duke of Gloucester and the Duke of Edinburgh. Queen Elizabeth later wrote to thank everybody who had offered tributes and kindness: 'Throughout our married life we have tried, the King and I, to fulfil with all our hearts and all our strength the great task of service that was laid upon us. My only wish now is that I may be allowed to continue the work that we sought to do together.'

1953-1959
QUEEN MOTHER

AFTER the funeral Queen Elizabeth endured a period of great private grief. However, there were important things to be done. As the Duke of Edinburgh once said, the monarch has to 'live above the shop,' and so Queen Elizabeth had to move out of Buckingham Palace and Balmoral for the Queen to move in. In May 1953, just before the coronation she went to Clarence House in St James's, with her household and Princess Margaret. She was delighted to be able to take over Birkhall on the Balmoral estate, for it was there that she and her husband had spent their summers before his accession. She also kept Royal Lodge, another place with happy memories.

Queen Mary had survived three of her sons and watched another renounce his throne and go into exile. On 24th March 1953 she died at Marlborough House, aged 85. She missed her granddaughter's coronation by less than three months. During her last years she felt she had to lead by example, and refused to heat her home. She had spent the war at Badminton revelling in the frugality of rationing, though she always wore jewellery for dinner. She was not at all a country person, and frequently picked up 'useless pieces of iron' in the fields intending to send them off for the war effort. These farm implements had to be subtly returned to the farm labourers. She also had an immensely generous side to her nature. Surplus items were always donated to charity bazaars. As a christening present she gave Prince Charles a silver gilt cup given by King George III to his godson in 1780. As she pointed out, it represented 168 years 'from my great grandfather to my great grandson'. All her life she had been interested in antiques, and towards the end was still visiting a museum or gallery every day. Early in 1953 she said to an old friend: 'I am beginning to lose my memory, but I mean to get it back.'

The Queen's coronation was the first to be televised, and over twenty million people watched it, while another twelve million heard it on the wireless. Queen Elizabeth attended it, just as Queen Mary had gone to her own son's in 1937. There were still things to be done. She realized that she couldn't lock herself away as other dowager queens had done. Even in May 1953 she was trying out the rather extreme method of taking one's mind off things by flying across Europe in one of the new Comet jet airliners. She even took the controls for a while. During the war she had become Honorary Air Commodore of 600 Squadron, the Royal Auxiliary Air Force, and she sent them a telegram the following day: 'I am delighted to tell you that today I took over as first pilot of a Comet aircraft. We exceeded a reading of 0.8 mach at 40,000 feet. Thoughts turned to 600 Squadron. What the passengers thought I really wouldn't like to say.' 'Your squadron overwhelmingly proud', came the reply.

'I found the Castle of Mey, with its long history, its serene beauty, and its proud setting, faced with the prospect of having no one to occupy it. I felt a great wish, if I could, to preserve this ancient dwelling.' Queen Elizabeth was introduced to Barrogill Castle, as it was then, ancient seat of the Sinclairs, in 1952 by Lady Vyner who lived nearby. It struck her that it would be a useful and, more importantly, absorbing task to restore it. The process, which included replacing the roof which blew off in gales that winter, took three years. The estate which went with it, Longoe Farm, now holds her herd of prize-winning Aberdeen Angus cattle. On a clear day, the view across the Pentland Firth, and the two whirlpools, the Twirlies and the Swirlies, reaches as far as the Old Man of Hoy in the Orkneys. The Castle of Mey itself holds no memories of the King, so nothing to excite her sadness and sense of loss. Most of the surviving contents of 145 Piccadilly are there though.

The Margaret Set consisted of high-livers like the Hon. Colin Tennant, the Marquis of Blandford, the Earl of Dalkeith, Lord Porchester, and the Hon. Peter Ward. However, Princess Margaret fell in love with Group Captain Peter Townsend, a member of her mother's household. Ultimately the couple were constitutionally thwarted in their affair, but it required considerable and tactful work by Queen Elizabeth to prove to them that it was impossible. Princess Margaret had to wait until she was twenty-five under the terms of the Royal Marriages Act before she could marry without the permission of the monarch, her sister. Townsend was sent to Brussels as Air Attaché for those two years. When he came back he and the Princess had to come to the conclusion that they had no future together. The Lord President of the Council and Conservative Leader in the House of Lords, Lord Salisbury, said that he would resign if Parliament was asked to approve the wedding. On 31st October 1955 Princess Margaret issued the following statement: 'I would like it to be known that I have decided not to marry Group Captain Peter Townsend. I have been aware that, subject to my renouncing my rights to succession, it might be possible for me to contract a civil marriage. But mindful of the Church's teaching that Christian marriage is indissoluble, and conscious of my duty to the Commonwealth, I have resolved to put these considerations before others. I have reached this decision entirely alone, and in doing so I have been strengthened by the unfailing support of Group Captain Townsend. I am deeply grateful for the concern of all those who have constantly prayed for my happiness.'

In the meantime Queen Elizabeth took Princess Margaret on a tour of Southern Rhodesia to attend the centenary celebrations of Cecil Rhodes' birth. They chose to go in the Comet aircraft that Queen Elizabeth enjoyed so much. The 'plane stopped at Rome, Beirut and Khartoum before becoming the first jet to land at the capital Salisbury. They went to Bulawayo where Queen Elizabeth opened the Central African Rhodes Centenary Exhibition in front of 25,000 people. 'The whole development has been that of a tiny white community surrounded by primitive Africans growing into a young and flourishing nation', Queen Elizabeth said in her speech.

In the autumn of 1954 she visited Canada and the United States, taking time to see her old friend and fellow widow Eleanor Roosevelt. At the time America was engaged in a hysterical campaign against communism, including the witch-hunt trials against people suspected of Un-American Activities, instigated by Senator Joe McCarthy. Britain, though, was more tolerant, and Queen Elizabeth boldly stated her country's case at a dinner at the Waldorf-Astoria in New York: 'We in Britain are perhaps too much disposed to judge American policy by the making of it, which frequently takes place in an atmosphere of considerable clatter. We do not always wait as confidently as we should for the final results, which are apt to be moderate, generous and wise. Similarly, people in the United States are inclined to misinterpret British policy, because we go about it in our own quite different way.'

Queen Elizabeth had been a racehorse owner since 1949. The popular amateur rider, Lord Mildmay of Fleet, persuaded her and Princess Elizabeth that they should look for something to go well over the sticks. Together they bought a steeplechaser, called Monaveen, which won the George Williamson Handicap by fifteen lengths. Sadly that first animal was later killed in a fall, after which the Princess turned her allegiance to the flat and steadfastly refused to own another steeplechaser. However Queen Elizabeth's stable never looked back, and in 1956 she had her first serious hope for the Grand National. Devon Loch, ridden by Dick Francis, now a famous author, was six lengths ahead and all fences jumped. The crowd were cheering madly when suddenly the horse simply collapsed, allowing ESB to become the luckiest winner ever. Devon Loch recovered a few minutes later, but no one knows what went wrong. Dick Francis was in tears, and Queen Elizabeth's first reaction was to go down and see that he and the beast were all right. 'That's racing,' was her only comment.

She went to Rhodesia and Nyasaland in 1957, just as the new British Prime Minister, Harold Macmillan, spoke of his famous Wind of Change. In 1958 she flew to Australia and New Zealand, stopping at Fiji on the way. In her 1927 tour her husband had downed the bitter-tasting national drink Kava, and now, to the delight of the islanders, so did she. On her return to Britain she gave a speech at a banquet in the Guildhall: 'One little family I saw in Australia had left their home near us in Scotland two years ago. The father had found a job he liked, the son loved the hard but rewarding life on a sheep station, the daughter was at a good school, and the mother was happy because of the great kindness they had received on all sides. I mention this as an example of the opportunities which await those who seek them in this rewarding land.'

After her visit to the Pope in 1959 – when she had to tell upset members of the Free Church of Scotland that, 'You will no doubt realize that a courtesy of this nature does not imply or reflect any views as to the political or religious opinions of the heads of state visitant', – she ended the decade by working a little magic in Africa. Mau Mau terrorists and Kenyan nationalists threatened to disrupt her trip. One member of the legislative council felt moved to say: 'If the Queen Mother does not find a warm welcome from Africans in Kenya, we hope she will understand it is because of the prevailing circumstances. It must not be taken as a sign of discourtesy or disloyalty.' When she arrived in the Masai capital of Narok, which was wracked by drought, she told the gathering: 'I hope you will be blessed with good rains.' As she walked to her car the heavens opened.

Page 92: On 7th March 1958 Queen Elizabeth was driven round Melbourne Cricket Ground in an open-top Land Rover at a gathering of 125,000 children, who cheered tremendously. This was ten times the size of the children's rally she and her husband had reviewed during their 1927 visit. Australian officialdom was terrified of the discipline problem, and this came to a head at the University of Melbourne. She had made her first speech on Australian soil at Sydney University, again in 1927, so was an old hand at Australian students, but in Melbourne over thirty years later the security was stringent in an effort to foil any practical jokes. 'It's a pity that the students are so quiet. Unless they reach an uncomfortable stage a student rag is fun', Queen Elizabeth remarked. 'Flour bombs are a little uncomfortable, of course', she added.

Queen Elizabeth and Princess Margaret at the coronation, with Prince Charles in the middle looking bored. The coronation, television, and Richard Dimbleby had an inestimable effect on each other. For the first time the splendour was being transmitted to every home; for the first time there was a reason to watch the nine-inch screen; and both these events would forever be associated with the BBC commentator who, according to Malcolm Muggeridge, should have been awarded the title Gold Microphone in Waiting. Another notable event of that day was the procession of the strongly-built Queen Salote of Tonga, who insisted on keeping the landau she was riding in to the Abbey open, despite the pouring rain. A tiny sultan from Kelantan in Malaysia shared it with her, shivering, and looking miserable, prompting Noel Coward's theory that he was probably her lunch.

The coronation of Queen Elizabeth II took place on 2nd June 1953. With typical 1950s faith in science and technology this date was chosen because, according to the meteorological office, it was the day least likely to rain. It rained. Following Queen Mary's lead at George VI's coronation, Queen Elizabeth attended her daughter's, even wearing Queen Mary's magnificent ermine-trimmed train. This picture shows the arrival of Queen Elizabeth's procession at Westminster Abbey. When the royal family came out onto the balcony at Buckingham Palace they made room in the middle for the Queen's consort, Prince Philip, to lead his mother-in-law out to tumultuous cheers. 'One must feel gratitude for what has been, rather than distress for what is lost', she said after her husband's death.

Queen Elizabeth and Prince Charles in *Y Bthwyn Bach* at Royal Lodge on 7th April 1954. This child-size house – fifteen feet high and with six rooms – is a perennial favourite with monarchs and their grandchildren. It was a present from the people of Wales to the Princesses Margaret and Elizabeth in 1932. King George V played with his granddaughter here, the Queen has been seen with her eldest grandson Peter Phillips and in this picture Queen Elizabeth is with Prince Charles. These latter have always had a close relationship, even at the age of five and fifty-three. A couple of years later Queen Elizabeth said of him: 'He is a very gentle boy. He has a very kind heart which, I think, is the essence of everything.'

Opposite: In October 1954 Queen Elizabeth embarked on one of her all-time great tours – to rank in importance with the 1927 world tour, the pre-war visit to the USA, and the 1947 tour of South Africa. The big difference was that this time she was alone. (As alone as a queen with her retinue can ever be.) She had been invited to the United States to receive money subscribed by the American people to the King George VI Memorial Fund for the training of young people of the Commonwealth. It was a twenty-three day tour, taking in New York, Washington and Boston. Having started quietly enough, it gathered momentum, as the crowds and press coverage increased, until it was front page news both sides of the Atlantic. There were banquets and balls, meetings with the Eisenhowers, the Nixons, ambassadors, mayors, the great and the good, and even Senator Joseph McCarthy. This charming picture was taken at a gala performance of the musical The Pyjama Game which was currently the hottest show on Broadway.

After the triumph of the visit to the United States, Queen Elizabeth spent a week in Canada where she was equally successful. It was seriously suggested that she should become Governor General as she was so popular with both the English and French-speaking Canadians. She has always maintained a special relationship with Canada and would probably have enjoyed the post, but the Queen is reputed to have rejected the proposal, saying 'I am afraid we could not do without her'. This picture, taken at Government House in Ottawa shows the glare of the enormous film lighting reflecting off the vast portraits of King George V and Queen Mary. In the days of Empire such vast canvasses were found in Government Houses and High Commissions all over the world. Today's portraits are more modest. Throughout her tour Queen Elizabeth made marvellous entrances to the banquets and dinners she attended, being preceded by three pipers, two of the Black Watch and her own Piper Major. They can be seen here, standing behind her.

Opposite: On 27th May 1954 at a special parade of 300 officers and men in the Inner Temple Garden Queen Elizabeth presented new colours to the Inns of Court Regiment. She had a double reason for making the presentation, for not only is she a bencher of the Middle Temple, but also Colonel-in-Chief of the 7th Hussars. It wasn't until 1935 that the right to carry colours was granted to the modern Inns of Court Regiment and provision for them was not authorised until 1953. In the interval the regiment ceased to be an infantry battalion and had become a yeomanry regiment, classified as hussars, in the reconstituted Territorial Army. The regiment is therefore unique in being not only the sole cavalry regiment entitled to carry infantry colours, but also the only regiment of hussars to carry colours of any description. Queen Elizabeth here shares a joke with Colonel C A Joss MC TD, on her arrival at the Inner Temple Garden. He appears to have got his sword into something of a twist, which I know, from my own days in the Guards, is not difficult to do.

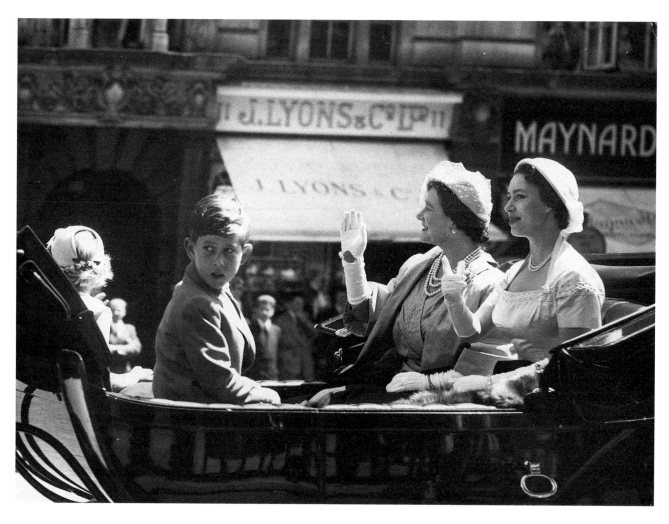

Queen Elizabeth, Princess Margaret, Prince Charles and
Princess Anne drive from Horse Guards Parade on 13th
June 1957 after the Queen's Birthday Parade. Queen
Elizabeth relished being a grandmother from the start.
She went to visit Prince Charles at Cheam whenever she
was allowed to, and when he went to Gordonstoun she
held tea parties for him and his friends aboard the royal
train in a nearby siding. She also taught him both the
sport of fishing and the pleasures of gardening. She
nurtured Princess Anne's riding, and was keen for her to
go to Benenden. Prince William of Gloucester once said,
'I can't tell you what the Queen Mother means to us all.
You only had to be loved by her, and to love her
yourself, to know that, no matter what, you could never
let her down.'

Opposite: On 22nd October 1957 the Queen and Prince Philip arrived back from a state visit to the United States. Here Queen Elizabeth points out their aeroplane to Princess Anne at Heathrow Airport. Queen Elizabeth had had a strenuous summer herself with visits to Rhodesia and Nyasaland, which had been joined together as a federation. Nyasaland later became Malawi, Northern Rhodesia Zambia, and Southern Rhodesia Zimbabwe. During the trip she went down a copper mine, became the first president of the University College of Salisbury, and addressed tribal chiefs, who called her *Mambo Kazi*, Big Mother – quite a compliment in southern Africa. She spoke to the assembled dignitaries about the need for cooperation between Africans and European settlers: 'When one ox pulls this way and the other that, nothing is achieved. It may even be that the yoke is broken. But when all bow their yokes the plough moves and the work for the harvest has begun.'

The Queen Mother arrives at a state reception for 1000 people in the Sydney Town Hall during her tour of the world in 1958. With her in this radiant group is the Premier of New South Wales, Mr J Cahill. After Sydney, where it was so hot that at one engagement twenty-one women were reported to collapse, she went to Brisbane, and from there she drove through the torrential rain which had the other half of Australia awash that year. The storms were so bad that the royal cavalcade missed the turnings to some towns and had to go back to try to find them. At one airstrip the gale was so strong that the wind yanked the ceremonial feathers out of the Governor's plumed helmet, and throughout the trip the ladies' hats were going up like clay pigeons. On another occasion the mistake was human rather than elemental when Queen Elizabeth asked her driver to slow down as they drove past a crowd. He abruptly slammed on the brakes and she was hurled to the floor in a tangle of ladies-in-waiting.

Opposite: Queen Elizabeth passes through crowds at a garden party at Wellington, New Zealand, on 14th February 1958. On this trip she became the first member of the royal family to fly around the world, though the Super-Constellation aeroplane which the royal party used broke down three times. On the last occasion the cylinder head cracked, and they had to make a three-day stop at Mauritius. The tour had originally been proposed for both her and George VI ten years before, and the route was much the same one that they had undertaken in 1927. Instead of six months away, though, it was only six weeks, but Queen Elizabeth only allowed herself one day to rest.

On her arrival at Canberra by air from New Zealand on 18th February 1958, Queen Elizabeth was received by the Prime Minister Mr Robert Menzies, later knighted, and the Governor General Sir William Slim (with his back to the camera). Sir Robert, who died in 1978, was Prime Minister of Australia from 1939 to 1941, when he brought the country into the Second World War, and then again from 1949 to 1966. He was an ardent anti-communist who propagated links with the United States and Britain. He later sent troops to fight in Korea and Vietnam. Sir William, who died in 1970, led the jungle campaign which recaptured Burma from the Japanese. In 1948 he became Chief of the Imperial General Staff and, from 1953 to 1960, was Governor-General of Australia.

On 20th February 1959 Queen Elizabeth arrived at Entebbe Airport and was welcomed to Uganda by the Kabaka of Buganda. They are pictured here at the Bulange, the headquarters of the Kabaka's government in Kampala, the capital. Buganda was a small self-governing state within the British colony of Uganda led by the Kabaka, Frederick Mutesa II. The wheels of independence within Uganda did not begin to turn until Sir Andrew Cohen was made Governor in 1952. However, it was ten years before Milton Obote was able to form his government. The Kabaka became President in 1963, but Obote, his Prime Minister, launched an attack on the Bulange in 1966, and the Kabaka was forced into exile. Having been ravaged by Idi Amin, Uganda is now high on the list of countries which the Princess Royal visits during her crusades for the Save the Children Fund. Of particular interest in this photograph is the Kabaka's intriguing choice of dress – a fine compromise between African and European.

1960-1969
FAVOURITE GRANDMOTHER

THE SIXTIES began with the birth, on 19th February, of Prince Andrew, and the death in the same month of the Marquess of Carisbrooke, who was Queen Victoria's last surviving grandson. Then Princess Margaret announced that she was to marry Anthony Armstrong-Jones. Their wedding was the most popular event in terms of numbers of people since the coronation. They went to the Caribbean on the royal yacht *Britannia* for their honeymoon, where the Hon. Colin Tennant gave Princess Margaret some land on the island of Mustique as a wedding present.

On 11th May, less than a week after her daughter's wedding, Queen Elizabeth went back once again to Rhodesia and Nyasaland to open the Kariba Dam. There she was presented with six emeralds from a local mine, and was cheered along her route by a crowd of 60,000. On a trip to Mount Zomba she collected specimens of a dozen wild flowers. She made a speech at a review of the British South African Police, saying, 'The spirit of courage and enthusiasm which created this great country I have felt to be as strong as ever. My prayer is that with growing understanding and good will you will build a future in which all can live in peace and happiness.'

She went to Tunisia in 1961, Canada the year after, but didn't leave the British Isles at all in 1963, except for private visits to France. Although a tour of Canada, Australia and New Zealand had to be cancelled for her to have an appendix operation, 1964 was an extraordinary year for Queen Elizabeth. Four royal births took place within eight weeks. Princess Alexandra, who had married Angus Ogilvy, gave birth to her first child, James, on 29th February, and three days later the Queen had Prince Edward. Lady Helen Windsor was born to the Duchess of Kent on 28th April, and finally, on 1st May, Princess Margaret bore her second child, Lady Sarah Armstrong-Jones. Queen Elizabeth went away for three weeks to cruise the Caribbean in *Britannia*.

She made her postponed grand tour of 1964 in 1966, and on the way from Australia to Canada during the 30,000 mile trip she danced the hula in Honolulu with Hawaii's Duke Kahanamoku at a reception given by the Governor, but she was back in hospital with another stomach complaint in December. She had a colostomy operation, performed by the Queen's surgeon, Sir Ralph Marnham, from South Africa, and King George VI's surgeon, the New Zealander, Sir Arthur Poritt. Members of Harold Wilson's government sent her a get well card as she languished in bed over Christmas, and she received up to 300 a day for weeks afterwards. It was here she learnt that what 'comfortable' means to the doctor is quite different from what it means to the patient. She was first seen in public on 22nd January when she went to morning service with the Queen at Flitcham near Sandringham. Her only other foreign tour was a fortnight in Canada in 1967.

She had to relax her schedule a bit. Her sister Rose, Countess Granville, died in November 1967 in the Forfar Hospital, making Queen Elizabeth the last surviving member of that generation of Bowes-Lyons. She gave up her Lord High Commissionership to the General Assembly of the Church of Scotland, which was especially frustrating since her husband had held exactly that post nearly forty years before. She did sail in the royal yacht to Normandy in 1967 to attend the 23rd anniversary of the D-Day landings, though. The Mayor of Gray, near Arromanches, presented her with the photograph of the King he had taken shortly after the Allies gained their foothold in Europe.

In 1968 she took her granddaughter, Princess Anne, to a party celebrating the British equestrian team's triumph of four gold medals at the 1968 Mexico Olympics. It was held at Whitbread's cellars in the City of London. Whitbread sponsor the Badminton Horse Trials. One of the reserve riders invited was Officer Cadet Mark Phillips, who was at Sandhurst at the time. Queen Elizabeth also went to see the *Queen Elizabeth* before the ship was withdrawn from Cunard's service. She was presented with a set of commemorative goblets at lunch in the Verandah Grill, by the Chairman of Cunard, and she talked to the ship's captain Commodore Geoffrey Marr. She had launched this liner thirty years earlier.

The royal family's last major public act of the 1960s was the investiture of Prince Charles as Prince of Wales at Caernarvon Castle on 1st July 1969, which was stage managed by Lord Snowdon who had become Constable of Caernarvon in 1963. He worked with Carl Toms, the stage designer, and John Pound of the Department of the Environment in an effort to keep the thirteenth century castle as serene and uncluttered a backdrop as possible. Over 200 million people watched it worldwide, though a group called the Free Wales Army said that they would try to foil any attempts to broadcast the event. They failed. Prince Charles, who has always had a special place in Queen Elizabeth's affections, now took on a far greater responsibility. He began by making a tour of Wales, a tour which was a major factor in the Welsh decision, a few years later, not to opt for devolution.

The 1960s saw the birth of most of modern photography from portraits to photojournalism. Newspaper supplements and womens' magazines increased the demand for colour pictures, but the media was confused by its own growth. Finding themselves faced with what seemed to be nothing other than lively chaos, the journalists decided to deal with it in the time-honoured way by concentrating on personalities; the gossip columns, and then the feature pages, and then even the headlines themselves were slowly taken over by a small and constantly shifting set of shakers and movers, the in-crowd, whose every thought and action was chronicled with a reverent solemnity that now seems deeply silly. These did not include members of the royal family who, in striking contrast with the 1980s, were not every other lensman's target.

Studio Lisa, now a part of the Hulton-Deutsch Collection, took this picture to commemorate Queen Elizabeth's sixtieth birthday. She is photographed at her desk in her private sitting room at Clarence House. She is wearing a blue and white lace dress with a platinum mink stole. Throughout her life she has been as strongly associated with pearls as the Princess of Wales is today. They are jewellery particularly appropriate to today's concern with the environment, for the oysters which produce them will only live in the most scrupulously unpolluted waters. The Queen and Princess Margaret also inherited a love for pearls, and were given their first necklaces by their grandfather, King George V, when he celebrated his silver jubilee in 1935. After her sixtieth birthday Queen Elizabeth flew to the Castle of Mey for her summer holiday.

Page 106: Prince Charles, Princess Anne and Prince Andrew visited Queen Elizabeth for her birthday in 1960. Prince Andrew, her third grandchild, born on 19th February 1960, is ten years younger than Princess Anne. He was named after his paternal grandfather, Prince Andrew of Greece, who in 1922 at King George V's instigation had been rescued by the destroyer *HMS Calypso* from a revolutionary committee in Athens. Queen Elizabeth said she was delighted that her new grandson was such a good-looking baby.

I would like to quote from a speech which Queen Elizabeth made in 1960. 'In the breathless pursuit of technical mastery we must not lose sight of something even more precarious, the true purpose of education, which is surely the making of human things by the training of three aspects of man – body, mind and character. The ages in which the world has made some of its greatest advances are those in which piety and vision have caught sight of levels higher than those on which the world is moving. Do not, therefore, in today's tumult, lose sight of the ancient virtues: service, truth and wisdom.'

A week after Prince Andrew's birth Princess Margaret announced her engagement to Anthony Armstrong-Jones, and they were married in Westminster Abbey on 6th May. On 8th December 1960, Queen Elizabeth, with Princess Margaret and her husband, who was created Lord Snowdon in 1961, went to the gala matinée of the ballet presented by the Royal Academy of Dancing, at the Theatre Royal, Drury Lane. Here they met Dame Margot Fonteyn and children of the Royal School of Dancing on stage after the performance. After her marriage Princess Margaret moved from Clarence House to a small house at Kensington Palace, once used by Lord Carisbrooke. When she began her family she took over 1a Clock Court, which was an entire wing of Kensington Palace, previously occupied in 1939 by the Duchess of Argyll, Princess Louise.

Queen Elizabeth went to Epsom on Oaks Day on 2nd June 1961. Less than two weeks after this picture she broke a small bone in her foot at Royal Lodge while there for Ascot. For the launching of the liner *Northern Star* at the Vickers-Armstrong factory on Tyneside she arrived in a wheelchair but rather than be lowered onto a special platform she limped down the ramp. She managed without the wheelchair when she received 200 American teachers, who were in Britain on an exchange programme, at Lancaster House a few days later, but had an hour of handshaking from a chair with her foot on a stool. At an agricultural show in Cambridgeshire she went between stalls in a wheelchair. The following year she broke the bone again at Birkhall.

Queen Elizabeth and Priness Anne at Horse Guards Parade for Trooping the Colour on 10th June 1961. Princess Anne was only ten at the time, but had already showed some of her lively and forthright character. The Duchess of Gloucester remembered her at the age of five plunging a knife into a guest's bed at Balmoral right through to the mattress. 'I've always wanted to do this,' she said. Queen Elizabeth was guilty of much the same crime at a similar age when she shredded her sheets at Glamis with a pair of scissors. Two years later Princess Anne went to Benenden, the girl's boarding school in Kent. She left to pursue her career in three-day eventing in 1968 with six 'O' levels and two 'A' levels.

Queen Elizabeth with Queen Fabiola of Belgium at the Royal Opera House, Covent Garden on 15th May 1963. King Baudouin and Queen Fabiola were on a state visit and the King was to be created a Knight of the Garter and appointed Honorary Air Chief Marshal of the Royal Air Force. Lord Drogheda who was managing director of the Royal Opera House, is in the background talking to the Duke of Edinburgh.

Queen Elizabeth at the Garter Ceremony in Windsor Castle in June 1962. The order of the Garter was constituted by King Edward III in 1348. Since 1831 it has been made up of the monarch and twenty four Knights Companions, and elected descendants of King George I. Extra knights can be admitted by special statute. The Prince of Wales is always invested with the Garter. The knights' uniform is extremely complicated. The garter itself is dark blue velvet, edged with gold, and bears the motto *Honi soit qui mal y pense* embroidered in gold. 'Evil on him who thinks bad of it,' is the translation of what King Edward said to his chortling assembled knights when Lady Salisbury's garter slipped off at a middle ages ball. It also has a buckle and a pendant of gold. It is worn just below the left knee. The mantle is dark blue velvet lined with white taffeta, the hood, with its white ostrich plumes, and surcoat are of crimson velvet and the hat is black velvet lined with white taffeta. The mantle bears a representation of the Garter around the Cross of St George on an escutchon argent on the left shoulder. A collar of gold weighing thirty troy ounces is worn. The eight-pointed star, which is made of silver has to be returned to the sovereign on the holder's death.

Queen Elizabeth attends the Garter ceremony at
Windsor on 14th June 1965. New knights are always
invested at Windsor before going on to a service in St
George's Chapel. Afterward the company process in
carriages to lunch at Windsor Castle. Windsor has been
a royal residence since the timber fortification put up by
William the Conqueror on this strategic site which
commands the Thames valley. Henry II built the first
stone building, and it has ever since symbolized the
indestructibility of the monarchy. For me it inevitably
brings back memories of early dancing lessons which my
sister and I attended there.

This is Queen Elizabeth, Prince Andrew, and the previous Princess Royal, who died in 1965, on the balcony of Buckingham Palace in 1964. Mary, the Princess Royal was born in 1897, the only daughter of King George V. In 1922 she married the 6th Earl of Harewood. The Prince of Wales, said of her in 1919: 'I don't feel that she is happy. If only she would confide in me I might be able to do something. But she never complains. The trouble is that she is far too unselfish and conscientious. That's why she was so overworked at her lessons. When my brothers and I wanted her to play tennis she used to refuse because she had her French translation to do, or she hadn't read *The Times* that day. Is that normal for a girl?'

From left to right in this picture taken on 15th February 1965 at the royal film performance of Lord Jim, adapted from Conrad's novel and directed by Richard Brooks, are Peter O'Toole, Daliah Lavi, Jack Hawkins and Queen Elizabeth. Peter O'Toole, born in 1932, shot to stardom with films like Kidnapped and Lawrence of Arabia. He is better known now for his private life. Daliah Lavi, born 1940, is an Israeli leading lady, and has appeared in films from many countries. Jack Hawkins was one of Britain's leading post-war film stars until he developed cancer of the throat in 1966. An operation meant that he lost the use of his voice.

In 1966, after this picture was taken, and when she had returned from New Zealand, Queen Elizabeth underwent an operation 'to relieve a partial obstruction of the abdomen'. This was a simple colostomy, which about 20,000 people have each year. However, this information was not announced at the time, and the public were fearful that they were being kept in the dark. The operation took place at the King Edward VII Hospital for Officers in London. The public were not satisfied, though, until they heard that she had been sitting up in bed watching the racing at Sandown Park on the television. She actually saw her horse Irish Rover become her 150th steeplechase winner.

Queen Elizabeth at a gala ballet performance at Covent Garden on 24th March 1965. She had just returned from Jamaica where she was conferred with a Doctorate of Letters from the University of the West Indies. She also made a private five-day visit to Canada that year. This is a particularly regal portrait and merits some discussion of the jewels she is wearing. The tiara is the Indian Tiara, made for Queen Victoria in 1853. It used to contain opals but was reset with rubies by Queen Alexandra in 1912. The rubies and the necklace were presented to the Prince of Wales in 1875 by Sir Jung Bahadore of Nepal.

On 14th November 1966 Queen Elizabeth met
Morecambe and Wise at the Royal Variety Performance.
Wayne Nugent is standing behind them. She ended up
helping Eric Morecambe when in 1976 the comedy duo
went to receive their OBEs. Before his operation, Eric's
legs were bad, and he was warned that he'd have to
stand and wait for a couple of hours at the ceremony.
Luckily, his old friend Dame Flora Robson thought of
writing to Queen Elizabeth. As Eric recalled: 'So when
it came to the day of the investiture, Ernie and I and a
very old man who was at least 106 were in a room just
off the throne room at Buckingham Palace while
everyone else was queueing up for their gongs. Flora
had got us into a little ante-room where we could sit
down while old men twice our age were walking past,
yards at a time.' Morecambe and Wise were just as
funny off-stage as on.

Queen Elizabeth, in her capacity as president of the
organization, was guest of honour at a party given by the
Women's Royal Voluntary Service in St James's Palace
on 6th December 1966. The party was to celebrate the
re-organization of the WRVS in London to fit into the
pattern of the new Greater London Council. It was a
long and complicated piece of work, involving the
regrouping of the ninety WRVS centres in the old
London County Council area into the 32 boroughs of
Greater London. In this picture, the royal corgi Bee is
hoovering up the cake crumbs after being fed by the
Dowager Marchioness of Reading, Chairman of the
WRVS, who is chatting to Queen Elizabeth. Bee was the
only breeding granddaughter of the Queen's first corgi
Susan whose pups stayed with the Queen.

Opposite: During a tour of Australia and New Zealand
Queen Elizabeth took time off to go fishing. Although
she had a blank day the first time she went out, the day
this picture was taken, 29th April 1966, she eventually
pulled in a two-pound rainbow trout from the Waikato
River near Wairakei, Auckland. 'It would have been
better to get one out of the deep freeze,' she said. This
antipodean tour was originally intended for 1964, but
was postponed for the Queen Mother to have an
appendicitis operation. She finally arrived in Adelaide on
23rd March in her capacity as patron of the arts festival.
She also went to see Prince Charles, who had just
started at Timbertop, part of Geelong Grammar School
in the State of Victoria, and they travelled to the Snowy
Mountains together for a private fishing trip.

Queen Elizabeth being received at Copenhagen Airport
on 1st February 1968 by King Frederik and Queen
Ingrid when she went to attend Princess Benedikte's
wedding. My mother, Queen Elizabeth's niece, married
King Frederik's second cousin, Prince Georg of
Denmark at Glamis Castle in 1950. King Frederik IX,
who was one year older than Queen Elizabeth, married
Queen Ingrid, the daughter of King Gustav VI of
Sweden. I remember photographing them in 1964 when
the King discovered that we had both been to the same
tattooist, Mr Birchett in the Waterloo Road. I have a
single discreet family seahorse; the King's torso was
ablaze with tattoos, and not just Birchett's.

Opposite: Queen Elizabeth went to the annual St Patrick's Day parade on 16th March 1969 and presented a shamrock to the Irish Guards, who were at that time stationed at the Victoria Barracks in Windsor. She also gave one to the regimental Irish Wolfhound mascot Fionn. Standing next to her is Field Marshal the Earl Alexander of Tunis, made Colonel of the regiment in 1947, who died exactly three months after this picture was taken. He had an extremely distinguished life. After Harrow he went to Sandhurst, and the First World War broke out almost immediately. He fought in France, was wounded three times, and mentioned in despatches five times. In 1931 he married Lady Margaret Bingham, daughter of the 5th Earl of Lucan. In 1935 at Loe-Agra and Mohmand he was mentioned in despatches twice, and again as Commander of the 1st Corps in 1940. He became Field Marshal and Supreme Allied Commander Mediterranean Theatre in 1944, and then ADC General to the King. He was Governor-General of Canada from 1946 to 1952, and Minister of Defence from 1952 to 1954. He was 74 years old when he died.

Queen Elizabeth attends the Order of the Thistle Installation at St Giles's Cathedral, Edinburgh, the chapel of the Order, on 26th May 1969. The date of the first Order of the Thistle ceremony is not known, but the Order was revived by King James II and VII in 1687. Its dress code is not quite as complicated as that of the Order of the Garter, but is equally not something one can simply slip into. There are sixteen knights in addition to the sovereign, unless any have been created by special statute, and they wear an eight-pointed silver star with St Andrew's cross in the centre, and a thistle in green on a gold background in the middle of that. The mantle is of green velvet and the hat, planted with osprey feathers, of black velvet. The order's motto is *Nemo me impune lacessit*, which means 'No-one safely provokes me'.

1970-1979
THE SNAPSHOT
SEVENTIES

*'The virtues of an ordinary life
in an extraordinary life.'*
The Times

AFTER the frenzy of the sixties, during which the media had been largely uninterested in the royal family, who were definitely not swingers, the publishing world increased its demand for pictures. There was a lot of interest in the investiture of Prince Charles in 1969, but the wedding of Princess Anne to Captain Mark Phillips in 1973 really sparked the keg, as it were. This instigated the arrival of the ubiquitous royal paparazzi, who began to hang from trees near Balmoral with their telephoto lenses in greater droves like roosting jackdaws. Even more annoying were the jackals who snapped at Badminton and Burleigh Horse Trials, hoping to capture royal breeches getting wet. They were told to 'Naff off'. However, the 1970s also began to see less of a monopoly of official royal photographers. Until that decade only a select few had been commissioned, such as Marcus Adams, Lord Snowdon and Cecil Beaton; and only one was in favour at a time. Suddenly a much larger group, including Norman Parkinson, Peter Grugeon, and myself were invited to take portraits. The move was towards a portrayal of a dignified yet more relaxed royal family. Gone were the theatrical backgrounds and Hollywood-inspired poses. A diversity of favourite photographers became established, and for various reasons. Norman Parkinson used skilful techniques to flatter his subjects, such as light angled from underneath, which softens peoples' chins, and the same is used in fashion photography today. He was, though, less conscious of background then Beaton had been. Snowdon's style was great simplicity. He would use one light, no frills at all, and include perhaps a corgi to lift the image from the stiff pictures of the past.

Previous queens who had reached her age had usually become completely reclusive, but this was not so for Queen Elizabeth. She carried on making friends, and meeting new people has always been her great forte. At one of the agricultural shows she attended in 1977, a small boy was presented to her. Quite unexpectedly he came out with: 'I've also met your daughter. Do you know she's the Queen?' 'Yes,' replied Queen Elizabeth. 'Isn't it exciting?'

After her seventieth birthday the Castle of Mey began to grow more important as a retreat. She took enormous interest in its garden, even though it stands only a few miles south of the windswept Orkney Islands. 'Sweet-pea' blues, lavenders and pinks are the colours most apparent in that garden, as they are in her clothes. Even the castle itself, which is built of Caithness stone, has a pink hue. The 1960s and 70s brought a greater use of colour photography as the Sunday colour supplements gathered speed, and pastel shades became her personal stamp. She was easily recognizable across the pre-parade paddock at Ascot simply from her dress.

This was the decade that Queen Elizabeth became a great-grandmother. Peter Phillips was born on 15th November 1977, the first child of Princess Anne and Captain Mark Phillips, both of whom, by now, had represented Great Britain in the equestrian three-day event at separate Olympic Games. Other royal firsts associated with this birth included it taking place in a hospital, St. Mary's Paddington, under the supervision of the Queen's gynaecologist Mr George Pinker. He was the first child born so close to the throne (fifth in line) without a title for 474 years, for his parents made a conscious decision at the time of their marriage to try to avoid the accolades which accompany the pressures of royalty. From an early age Peter has displayed an aptitude for riding, though with parents like his it would be difficult not to. Fifty-two hours after he appeared another royal birth took place when the Duchess of Gloucester had Lady Davina Windsor.

1972 was a bad year with the deaths of King Frederik of Denmark, Prince William of Gloucester in an aircraft crash, and Alexander Ramsay, who was the husband of Princess Patricia of Connaught. However, it was also the year that Prince Richard of Gloucester married, and it was the Queen's silver wedding anniversary. To celebrate this latter there was a thanksgiving service at Westminster Abbey followed by a lunch at the Guildhall held by the Lord Mayor of London.

Tragedy struck most profoundly at the end of the decade when Lord Mountbatten of Burma, who was only a month older than Queen Elizabeth, was blown up on Monday 27th August 1979 while sailing in his boat *Shadow V* off the coast of Ireland. His grandson Nicholas Knatchbull and the seventeen-year-old boatman Paul Maxwell were also killed instantly, and the Dowager Lady Brabourne died of her injuries the next day. Lord and Lady Brabourne survived, as did Timothy, Nicholas's twin brother. It was during the Mountbatten family holiday, unchanged for thirty years, at Classiebawn Castle in County Sligo. On the same day eighteen soliders of the Queen's Own Highlanders and the Parachute Regiment were killed by the IRA in an ambush. Three days later the bodies of the Earl, Lady Brabourne, and Nicholas Knatchbull were taken to Dublin and flown by RAF Hercules to Eastleigh in Hampshire. The coffins were driven, accompanied by a guard of honour, Prince Charles and Prince Philip, to Broadlands. They stayed there, guarded by estate workers until 3rd September, when the Earl's body was taken to lie in state at Romsey Abbey, where he was eventually buried in the south transept, facing the sea. The funeral service itself was at Westminster Abbey, and Prince Charles read the lesson. One of the most abiding images of that day was Lord Mountbatten's horse, Dolly, whom he had ridden at the Trooping of the Colour just two months earlier, led behind the funeral cortège, with her master's boots reversed in the stirrups.

Page 120: On her seventieth birthday Queen Elizabeth stands with three of her grandchildren, Lady Sarah Armstrong-Jones, Prince Edward and Viscount Linley. This picture, when the press at large traditionally have a kind of official photocall on her birthday, continues the theme of the garden that Beaton began with his portraits. The Marchioness of Salisbury who is an expert gardener and a personal friend of Queen Elizabeth once noted that Her Majesty's four gardens, at Royal Lodge, the Castle of Mey, Clarence House, and Birkhall, are linked in atmosphere by the four harmonious strands of attention, love, knowledge and personal taste.

Queen Elizabeth's interest in horses includes three-day eventing. The Duke of Beaufort's seat, Badminton, hosts the most famous trials. The most notable Badminton of the 1970s was in 1973 when the Queen presented her future son-in-law Captain Mark Philips with the Whitbread trophy and two commemorative plaques. The Queen owned Columbus, the horse which he rode, and Princess Anne came fourth on Goodwill to complete the royal hat-trick. In this picture, a typical snap of the period, Queen Elizabeth is watching the cross country. Her host, old friend and former Master of Horse, the 10th Duke of Beaufort, who was only four months older than she, died in 1984. It was he who inaugurated the three day event in April 1949 and built it up to be perhaps the premier trials of its kind outside the Olympics. Queen Elizabeth also regularly stays at Badminton for the Cheltenham races, particularly the Gold Cup.

Queen Elizabeth at ease with Lord and Lady Harlech, on 21st September 1970 at the world première of The Lament of the Waves at the Royal Opera House, Covent Garden. Lord Harlech was well known as President of the British Board of Film Censors. His signature was at the beginning of all films at the cinema. He was also an expert on British foreign policy and British ambassador to the USA, but sadly he died in a car crash in 1985. Queen Elizabeth, who has always been a great patron of the arts, has a very gregarious taste. She chose a selection of recordings for Radio 4 to play on her 85th birthday including comedy from the Crazy Gang, an extract from Private Lives by Noel Coward, and ITMA. She and the Prince of Wales attended a Rostropovitch concert at the Kings Lynn Festival, of which she is patron, and which until 1988 was organized by her lady-in-waiting Ruth, Lady Fermoy. Once a year, the harpsichordist, the late Tom Goff, used to hold a musical soirée for Queen Elizabeth at his house in Chelsea, and she has always been a keen dancer, especially the Highland variety, once persuading Lord Hailsham to discard his walking sticks for a reel.

Queen Elizabeth is here visiting the South of England Agricultural Society annual show at Ardingly in June 1970, wearing typically pastel-coloured clothes. She is accompanied by the Marquess of Abergavenny, Lord Lieutenant of East Sussex. Farming has always been an interest, and she is an Honorary Life Member of the Royal Agricultural Society. Attached to the Castle of Mey is the 120-acre Longoe Farm. The farm manager, Mr Donald McCarthy, under Queen Elizabeth's auspices, looks after a herd of Aberdeen Angus cattle, and North Country Cheviot sheep. Cannon Ball the bull won the supreme beef championship at the Caithness County Show in both 1976 and 1977, and in 1977 and 1978, a ram which she owned jointly with a neighbouring farmer was overall breed champion at the Royal Highland Show, and in 1977 reserve supreme sheep champion. At the Royal Smithfield Show in 1989, her Aberdeen Angus heifer won first prize.

Queen Elizabeth at Carpenters' Hall in London in 1972 greeting Queen Juliana of the Netherlands who is wearing the Garter sash and star which she received in 1958. This was a state visit, and she was also received by the Lord Mayor of London Sir Edward Howard. Queen Juliana, who abdicated her throne on 30th April 1980 in favour of her daughter Beatrix, is nine years younger than Queen Elizabeth. She also has the title Queen Mother and is like a cosy grandmother. She is so kind and unaffected that it is sometimes difficult to remember how royal she is. In May 1940 Juliana had to flee her country with her mother, the then Queen Wilhelmina, as Holland was overrun by the Germans in five days of bitter fighting. Wilhelmina headed her government in exile, and Prince Bernhard, Juliana's husband, was appointed Supreme Commander of the Netherlands Army and Air force, and of the Resistance organizations. The family returned in April 1945, just before liberation. In 1948 Wilhemina abdicated in favour of her daughter Juliana, who succeeded with the words 'Who am I to be worthy of this?' which will always remain impressed in the memory of the Dutch people.

Cecil Beaton's portrait of Queen Elizabeth, for her seventieth birthday, in the garden of Royal Lodge at Windsor, shows to the full his great feel for background by reflecting her love of gardening. If I am to be slightly critical I think it is a pity he has concentrated so much on the background that he has had to cut off the Queen Mother's hands and the flowers she is holding. The garden at Royal Lodge represents stability in a world of change. It has been Queen Elizabeth's wish to maintain it more or less exactly the same since her husband's death, for he helped her plan it. Five people work to make this garden as beautiful as it is. John Bond, who is managing director of Savill and Valley Gardens, supervises the roses and the ever-burgeoning undergrowth of the woodland garden on a consultancy basis, and Paddy Bennett is the permanent head gardener, with three other men under him, who look after everything else.

Photographs of the royal family together, or at least several members at a time, are rare. This is my own, and was something of a struggle to take. I had seen a Winterhalter painting of Queen Victoria surrounded by her children and saw no reason why I shouldn't be able to achieve the same with a camera. In 1971 the Queen very kindly asked me to Christmas at Windsor Castle. I decided to take the picture after lunch on Boxing Day. All my complicated plans were dashed when firstly I discovered that the drawing room was undergoing structural repairs, so I had to squeeze everybody into a corner, secondly, I fused all the lights whilst setting up, and thirdly some monster had sneaked in and switched round all my carefully laid out place cards. At last I was on top of the ladder shooting away, when I suddenly noticed that my assistant's head was reflected in the large mirror at the back, and so faithfully captured on celluloid. Thankfully, Lord Snowdon suggested that as a fail-safe I should abandon the ladder, take three separate shots with my feet on the ground, and paste those pictures together later in the studio. I did just that, resting my camera on a television. The Marx Brothers were on, and every time Groucho opened his mouth I released the shutter. To see where the picture was cut, look at where all the heads are looking, and bear in mind that I superimposed heads from other pictures in the set on those I wasn't happy with. I'm sure Winterhalter had an easier job with the painting.
Back row: The Earl of Snowdon, the Duchess of Kent with Lord Nicholas Windsor, the Duke of Kent, Prince Michael of Kent, the Duke of Edinburgh, the Prince of Wales, Prince Andrew, and the Hon. Angus Ogilvy.
Middle row: Princess Margaret, Queen Elizabeth, the Queen, the Earl of St. Andrews, Princess Anne, Marina Ogilvy, Princess Alexandra, James Ogilvy.
Front Row: Lady Sarah Armstrong-Jones, Viscount Linley, Prince Edward, Lady Helen Windsor.

Princess Anne married Captain Mark Phillips in November 1973. Norman Parkinson took this picture, and it is worth comparing with similar pictures from the 1980s. Glare is visible from the blisteringly hot tungsten lights, which used to turn the throne room into something approaching a film set. These days the same shot would be taken using a synchronized flash, and halogen lamps. A lot of people are blinking, and Prince Klaus of the Netherlands to the left of the couple is even looking away. The Queen Mother, as always, looks marvellous.

From left to right, the wedding guests in this picture are – Children: James Ogilvy, Prince Edward, Lady Sarah Armstrong-Jones, Marina Ogilvy, Viscount Linley, Lady Helen Windsor, The Earl of St Andrews.

Middle row: Crown Princess Beatrix of the Netherlands, Ex-King Constantine of Greece, Prince Klaus of the Netherlands, Princess Alice Countess of Athlone, Queen Anne-Marie of Greece, Sarah Phillips, Crown Prince Harald of Norway, Queen Margrethe II of Denmark, the Duchess of Kent, Captain Phillips, Princess Anne, the Queen, Princess Alice Duchess of Gloucester, Queen Elizabeth, Princess Margaret, Queen Sophie of Spain (obscured), Prince Andrew, the Earl of Snowdon, King Juan Carlos I of Spain, Prince Michael of Kent.

Back row: Major and Mrs Peter Phillips, Princess Alexandra, Captain Eric Grounds, the Hon. Angus Ogilvy, the Duke of Edinburgh, Princess Richard of Gloucester, Prince Richard of Gloucester, the Duke of Kent, the Prince of Wales, Earl Mountbatten of Burma.

Although corgis are her dogs, the Queen is a highly respected breeder of labradors, and keeps kennels at Sandringham. She also breeds cocker spaniels. Here she accompanies her mother at the North of Scotland Gun Dog Association Open Stake Retriever Trials at Balmoral in August 1973. Queen Elizabeth doesn't own any labradors but her attentions are not strictly confined to corgis either. She is president of the Dachshund Association. She doesn't enjoy shooting, though she hosts clay pigeon shoots at the Castle of Mey. King George VI was a fine shot, and always kept a full kennel of yellow labradors.

From left to right Queen Elizabeth wearing a lavender-colour dress, Prince Michael of Kent who was an usher, Princess Margaret in orange, the Duchess of Kent and the then Princess (later Queen) Beatrix of Holland leave Westminster Abbey after the wedding of my sister, Lady Elizabeth Anson, to Sir Geoffrey Shakerley on 27th July 1972. Among her bridesmaids were Lady Sarah Armstrong-Jones, and Princess Anne, who had by now been a bridesmaid at no less than six weddings. Other guests not in the picture included the Queen, the Duke of Kent, and Princess Margaretha of Sweden with her husband John Ambler. My sister Elizabeth is a great party organizer. Her company Party Planners arranged the celebrations after the weddings of both Prince Charles and Prince Andrew.

Official birthday portraits are taken quite a long time before the actual birthday. They have to be approved before being issued to the media about a month before publication. This picture, though, was actually taken on the Queen Mother's 75th birthday in the garden of Clarence House, by George Freston of Fox Photos. For many years George was one of only two press photographers trusted by the royal family to record events inside the royal homes on behalf of the entire world's press. The other, Ronald Bell, is Court Photographer for the Press Association.

Opposite: This is Norman Parkinson's portrait of Queen Elizabeth, issued for her 75th birthday. She is wearing a formal gown of white chiffon embroidered with gold beads. The necklace is pearl and diamond and was originally given to Princess Alexandra by the then Prince of Wales in 1863. The diamond tiara, which matches the bracelet, was made in the 1940s, and was slightly altered by Cartier in the 1950s. The diamond drop earrings were brought by the East India Company for Queen Victoria from Lahore in 1851. Just visible on her left shoulder is Queen Victoria's bar brooch which Queen Elizabeth is wearing vertically instead of horizontally.

This is a fabulous picture of life from Queen Elizabeth's point of view. She is waving at crowds outside Clarence House on the occasion of her 75th birthday (which she had hoped to spend quietly). Note how the eye is naturally drawn from the policeman keeping watch, through Queen Elizabeth, to the little girl in the front row with the camera. *The Times* tribute to her that morning ran: 'The Queen Mother has displayed the virtues of ordinary life in an extraordinary life.' One of her favourite birthday presents that year was from her old friend Benjamin Britten: an album of seven of Robert 'Robbie' Burns's poems, complete with the music for harp accompaniment by Britten himself. August 4th has become established as one of *the* dates in the royal calendar.

Queen Elizabeth keeps in almost daily contact with her trainer, Fulke Walwyn. The post used to be held by Major Peter Cazalet, but sadly he died in 1973 after twenty-five years of training her horses. This beast of hers is Sunnyboy, bought from Lady Beaverbrook, and it had just romped home to win the Fernbank Hurdle Race at Ascot on 18th February 1976 to bring her total of winners to 300, though these days the total stands at nearer 500. 'I'm so thrilled, and especially delighted that it should happen at Ascot. Thank you so much', she told her jockey, Bill Smith. 'It's a great milestone for her, and the greatest day in my career', he commented later. She was even more pleased to discover that one of her gardeners had backed it. One of her most famous pieces of equipment is 'The Blower', a line into Clarence House with all the information on runners, riders and starting prices from around the country, issuing commentaries like those which feed betting shops.

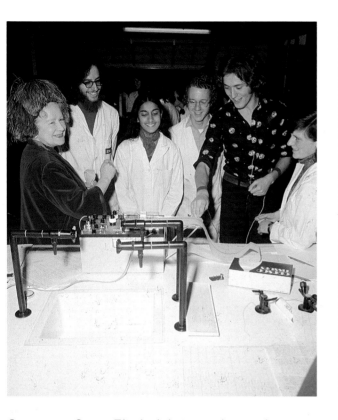

One reason Queen Elizabeth leaves such a good impression with people is the delighted interest she takes in what they do, such as here, at the opening of a new biology laboratory at Queen Mary College in the East End of London on 24th February 1976. Queen Elizabeth became Chancellor of the University of London in 1955. Her private secretary, Sir Martin Gilliat, called it 'The spark which set off her tumultuously varied way of life'. She was always on the side of the students, whom, she once said, 'are all too often in the headlines', but who only really want to study.

Queen Elizabeth, who refers to her stole and diamonds as 'my props', and Princess Margaret attend a gala performance of the ballet Mayerling at the Royal Opera House, Covent Garden in February 1978 accompanied by Sir Claus Moser.

I like the angle of this picture taken at Covent Garden on 30th May 1977. Queen Elizabeth is wearing two Royal Family Orders, the most personal mark of royal favour, the Order of George VI and the Order of Queen Elizabeth II. The first consists of a miniature of His Majesty, in the uniform of Admiral of the Fleet, set within an oval diamond border, surmounted by the Imperial Crown on a pink riband. The second is a miniature portrait of The Queen painted by Dorothy Wilding. This, again, is bordered by diamonds and surmounted by the Imperial Crown, but it is made of Chartreuse yellow watered silk.

Trooping the Colour brings most of the royal family together, and here Queen Elizabeth rides in an open landau with Princess Margaret in June 1979. Trooping the Colour is an old ceremony dating back to when the only identification a soldier had of what side he was on was the standard or 'colour' which preceded him into battle. Thus these colours became almost sacred. A different regiment each year Troops the Colour on the sovereign's official birthday. The seven regiments which make up the Household Division are the Welsh Guards, the Irish Guards, the Grenadier Guards, the Coldstream Guards the Scots Guards, the Life Guards and the Blues and Royals.

By the end of the seventies, Queen Elizabeth was unquestionably the first lady of steeplechasing. She had owned over sixty individual winning horses and had won over 330 races. In this picture, however, she is presenting, rather than receiving, the cup, The Horse and Hound Trophy, which is competed for by amateur riders. Her Majesty's enthusiasm for 'the winter game' is highly infectious.

Queen Elizabeth in the garden of the Castle of Mey with her friend and garden designer, Lady Salisbury, author of a stunning book, *The Gardens of Queen Elizabeth*. Although Her Majesty's interests are wide and varied, the two pictures on this page represent the two activities in which she most actively participates.

1980-1990
ROYAL
OCTOGENARIAN

'One of those extraordinarily rare people
whose touch can turn anything to gold.'
Prince Charles

AFTER her eightieth birthday celebrations, the two great royal occasions of the decade were the glittering weddings of her grandsons Prince Charles and Prince Andrew. The first match was especially pleasing for Queen Elizabeth, for the Princess of Wales is the granddaughter of her old friend, and lady-in-waiting since 1956, Ruth, Lady Fermoy. Lady Diana Spencer spent the night before her wedding at Clarence House, and woke early on the morning to be prepared by a small army of hairdressers and couturiers. Queen Elizabeth, dressed in eau-de-nil, left at 10.22 am with Prince Edward, who with Prince Andrew was one of Prince Charles's supporters, the royal equivalent of a best man. Exactly fifteen minutes later the bride left with her father, Lord Spencer, in the Glass Coach, for the journey to St Paul's Cathedral. Great sections of the pews were taken up by Prince Philip's vast family, and a strong Bowes-Lyon contingent was present, many of whom had not seen each other for years.

The music was provided by three choirs and three orchestras as well as the soprano Kiri te Kanawe. The bride's and bridesmaids' dresses were made of English silk, and the wedding ring was of Welsh gold. All was lavish. Even the flower arrangements were six feet wide and ten feet high. The Archbishop of Canterbury took the service, the Speaker of the House of Commons read the lesson, and prayers were said by the head of the Roman Catholic Church in Britain and the Moderator of the Church of Scotland. After the official photographs at Buckingham Palace, which I managed to take in under the eighteen minutes allowed, following careful planning and playing with scale models of all the dignitaries involved the night before, the Prince and Princess of Wales went out onto the balcony, where they kissed in front of the estimated one million people who packed London's streets, let alone those watching on television. Kings, queens and heads of state from all over the world attended. One similarity between the Queen's coronation and Prince Charles's wedding was the size of the sovereign of Tonga. In 1953 it had been the enormous Queen Salote. Now her son, the 26 stone King Taufa 'Ahautopou IV of Tonga, came – with his own chair.

The next royal wedding, which took place at Westminster Abbey on 23rd July 1986, was that of Prince Andrew and Sarah Ferguson, the second daughter of Major Ronald Ferguson, polo manager to the Prince of Wales. As the bride confidently predicted, no one had ever seen a dress like it. Again the heads of state and monarchs turned up and filed into their diplomatically allotted pews. Again The Mall was filled with people waiting for Prince Andrew to kiss the bride, and as before their hope was rewarded.

In between these two joyous occasions, Britain was involved once again in war. Argentina invaded the Falkland Islands and Prince Andrew went out with the task force as a helicopter pilot attached to *HMS Invincible*. After the thankfully brief conflict was over, he spoke about his experiences. Part of his job was to act as a decoy for Exocet missiles. These weapons only fly under a height of twenty-seven feet, so the idea is to attract them away from ships, and then gain height as they draw near. 'But on the day that *Sheffield* was hit, one Exocet was seen to fly over the mast of a ship, that is, well over twenty-seven feet. For the first ten minutes we didn't really know which way to turn or what to do. I knew where I was, and I was fairly frightened.' The other problem was the alarming way that the British Sea Wolf missiles would lock onto British helicopters by mistake. 'They locked onto the helicopter three times when we were hovering. It really makes your hair stand up on the back of your neck. It's not much fun at all having one of those fellows pick you out as a target.' Of his own squadron he said: 'Absolutely fantastic. They've worked very hard, and I can only say that the squadron is a great squadron, and I'm glad I've served with her.' Other members of the forces praised Prince Andrew's actions when picking up survivors of the *Atlantic Conveyor*, and the missing crew of one of *HMS Hermes* helicopters. Queen Elizabeth is keen on helicopters, and was the first member of the royal family to travel in one in 1956. The Queen, however, is not so enthusiastic, disliking the racket they make.

Queen Elizabeth lightened her load of royal duties this decade. She would still carry out nearly the same amount of engagements, but they would be of a less strenuous variety. She began to concentrate on her especially favourite jobs, like her regiments, which are 1st the Queen's Dragoon Guards, The Queen's Own Hussars, 9th/12th Royal Lancers (Prince of Wales's), the King's Regiment, the Royal Anglian Regiment, the Black Watch, the RAMC, and the Gordon Highlanders to name just the British ones. She would also support the Queen in state ceremonials, providing still invaluable experience for dealing with foreign leaders. She usually undertakes at least one tour a year. Despite threats from the IRA she went to Northern Ireland in 1983 to take the salute at the 75th anniversary parade of the Territorial Army at St Patrick's Barracks, Ballymena. She terrified her security organizers by wandering over to a crowd of people and chatting to them after planting a tree at Hillsborough Castle. That, incidentally, had been where her sister Rose lived while her husband Lord Granville was Governor of Northern Ireland. Their butler, Mr Harpur, was still there. In 1984 she visited the Channel Islands, in 1985 it was Venice and Canada, and a strenuous tour of the West Country aboard *Britannia* in 1986. 1987 saw her in Canada, and again in 1989, when she had a quite remarkable trip revisiting many of the places she had seen with the King fifty years previously.

She is extremely fit for her age, and seldom ill, despite the pressures of public life. She does lodge the odd fishbone in her throat, though. 'The salmon's revenge,' she once joked.

Page 136: This is a typical picture by Lord Snowdon, taken at Clarence House in 1987 for Queen Elizabeth's birthday. The one light, no frills approach only works in the most expert hands. She wears the necklace which she has owned since George VI's accession, and which was originally given to Princess Alexandra by the Prince of Wales in 1863. Her tiara is from the 1940s, but Cartier added the triangle motif to it in the 1950s. The light comes off both of them perfectly, and off the gilding on the chair. The sleepy corgi is called Ranger, the latest in many generations starting with Dookie in 1933.

The royal family on the balcony of Buckingham Palace after the Queen's Birthday Parade in June 1980, where it is obvious from the Queen's 'St Patrick's' blue plume that the Colour of the Irish Guards was being trooped. The Queen is pointing out to her two-year-old grandson Peter the RAF flypast. Amongst the royal party are Prince and Princess Michael of Kent, Princess Alexandra, the Duchess of Gloucester with her son Alexander Earl of Ulster, and Princess Sirindhorn of Thailand.

For Queen Elizabeth's eightieth birthday, stamps were issued by the General Post Office throughout the Commonwealth. They consisted of various portraits from 1904 onwards, and show scenes from her life in much the same vein as this book. We have room to show only six of these sets. Of the others, Nune, in the South Pacific, chose to use her coat of arms instead of a picture of her, and the one from Lesotho has an inset of a stamp issued in 1947 when King George VI and Queen Elizabeth visited Basutoland, as it used to be called.

At the thanksgiving service for Queen Elizabeth's eightieth birthday, on 15th July 1980, representatives of both the Church of Scotland and the Catholic Church said prayers, though it was conducted by the Archbishop of Canterbury. Dr Runcie later said that it was the most beautiful service he had ever taken. He finished his appreciative address with the words: 'Thank you Your Majesty. Thanks be to God.' At one stage in the proceedings Prince Charles and Princess Anne in the foreground had the most dreadful attack of giggles, and these were so thinly stifled that they were clearly audible to people who were standing nearby. In this picture you can see Prince Andrew looking across to see what the joke is, and there I am, standing two rows behind him, also looking slightly quizzical.

Queen Elizabeth and Prince Charles are returning in the
1902 State Landau to Buckingham Palace following her
eightieth birthday thanksgiving service. The celebrations
for this event began a few days before with a garden
party at the Palace of Holyroodhouse, Edinburgh,
followed by a musical tribute. The next day bands of the
Highland regiments played for an hour in her honour,
and in the evening there were Scottish reels at a
reception in Holyroodhouse. Then to London for the
service, where the Queen waived her prerogative of
arriving last and leaving first, so that her mother could
have a sovereign's escort. Two days later there was a
garden party at Buckingham Palace for representatives of
the three hundred organizations and charities with which
Queen Elizabeth is associated.

This family group was taken after the thanksgiving service. Other celebrations included a special performance of the Royal Tournament at Earls Court by her own military units. They also played the tune Castle of Mey composed in her honour. During the morning of her birthday more than 200 bouquets arrived at Clarence House as well as sackfuls of mail. Twelve Jet Provosts from the RAF Central Flying School of which she is Commander-in-Chief flew over at noon in an E formation. That evening she went to the première of the ballet Rhapsody which had been specially choreographed by Sir Frederick Ashton. Queen Elizabeth was delighted with this birthday present. It ended with a boisterous Happy Birthday, a more formal National Anthem, and silver rain pouring onto the cast. Afterwards on stage she blew a single candle out on a vast white and pink birthday cake, baked for her by Warrant Officer Bob Smith of the Army Catering Corps.

Left to right standing: Captain Mark Phillips, Prince Edward, Prince Charles, Duke of Edinburgh, Lady Sarah Armstrong-Jones, Viscount Linley.

Seated: Princess Anne, Queen Elizabeth, the Queen, Princess Margaret.

This charming picture of Queen Elizabeth and the Queen outside Clarence House on 4th August, her Majesty's eightieth birthday, won the Martini Royal Photographer of the Year Award for Anthony Marshall of the *Daily Telegraph*. I helped to found this competition in 1976 and I believe that it has been instrumental in improving the quality of royal photography since then. There is no doubt at all that, in particular, the standard of amateur photography of the royal family has changed beyond all recognition, and today there is very little to separate the winning amateur pictures from the winning professionals. On more than one occasion in recent years amateur photographers have beaten professionals in the competition. We also like to think it keeps intrusive pictures down to the minimum, for photographers know that if they misbehave they have no chance of winning.

Opposite: Unusual to shoot through a window though it is, Norman Parkinson has succeeded with this eightieth birthday portrait because of the great back lighting. This picture, taken at Clarence House, formed a central part of an exhibition of her pictures and portraits at the National Portrait Gallery. Age has never been allowed to be a valid excuse, or even a real concern for Queen Elizabeth. Queen Mary complained on reaching eighty: 'It's so tiresome getting old.' When Queen Elizabeth became an octogenarian Prince Charles suggested that perhaps this Octogen stuff was some sort of elixir used by great grandmothers to encourage and fortify all those around them.

For the most famous of Parkinson's eightieth birthday portraits he had these satin capes specially made. However it is the expressions on the faces which make this picture. It was taken at an extremely jolly photographic session where, by Princess Margaret's admission, the jokes were flying. Parkinson has said that this picture will go down in history for being timeless, since it cannot be dated by fashion. 'It was their idea', he added. As a fitting prelude to her eighties, Queen Elizabeth was appointed Lord Warden and Admiral of the Cinque Ports and Constable of Dover Castle. For the extremely elaborate ceremony she sailed down the Thames to Dover Castle in *Britannia* on 1st August 1979 where she swore to 'maintain the franchises, liberties, customs and usages of the ports'. She is the first woman ever to hold the title, previously held by the famous Duke of Wellington, Winston Churchill and Sir Robert Menzies.

Opposite: Every year, on 29th May, a member of the royal family visits the Royal Hospital Chelsea to celebrate Founder's Day. The hospital was founded by Charles II and the day is also known as Oak Apple Day, the statue of King Charles II being decorated with oak leaves to mark the famous occasion when that king took refuge amongst the branches of an enormous oak tree at Boscober, after the battle of Worcester. The hospital houses retired servicemen and NCOs who live out their last years in peace, wearing uniforms designed in the days of the great Duke of Marlborough. The Chelsea Pensioners have a reputation for living to a great age, no doubt due to the tranquility and beauty of the hospital which was designed by Sir Christopher Wren, with additions by Robert Adam and Sir John Soane. Our picture was taken in 1981 when there were still a number of Chelsea Pensioners who were considerably older than their royal visitor.

I myself took this picture of Zara Phillips's christening at Windsor Castle on 27th July 1981. It was only two days before the Prince of Wales's wedding at which I was to take the official pictures, so the preparations were all done in a bit of a rush. One of the surprises of the day was how low the Queen's sofa was! The people standing in the picture are Hugh Thomas the Olympic three-day eventer, Helen Stewart wife of motor racing ace Jackie, Major and Mrs Peter Phillips, the Duke of Edinburgh, the Countess of Lichfield who is an extra lady-in-waiting to the Princess Royal, and Colonel Andrew Parker-Bowles. Seated are Mark Phillips, the Queen, Princess Anne with Zara, Peter, Queen Elizabeth and Prince Andrew.

Almost everyone can remember what they were doing on
29th July 1981. I had prepared thoroughly for the
photography, but as I drove from my flat in Eaton
Square to the back of Buckingham Palace I was rigid
with fear. My assistants Chalky and Dawkins looked
uncomfortable in their morning dress and I am certain
that, like me, they wished they were somewhere else as
the earth-shaking roar of the crowd increased in volume
with the processions' return from St Paul's. You can
almost hear the cheering in this picture of Queen
Elizabeth and Prince Andrew in the Mall. As it was
taken I was watching the scene on television, conscious
that photographs like this would be on their way to the
world's picture editors before my own shutter had
moved. It also struck me that despite the *vorsprung
durch technik* of modern photography, the weight of the
necessary equipment for press photographers in the
street hardly changes. The lensman of the 1950s carried
a sixty pound battery to power that new invention the
electronic flash, as well as a camera bag. Many of these
people now complain of back trouble. Today they would
be staggering under an inventory including several
camera bodies loaded with different types of film, heavy
lenses, tripod, battery pack, field telephone and step
ladder.

This picture of mine, taken on that famous day 29th July 1981, was not easy. Because of the timing of the day I had a mere eighteen minutes to complete the set, so a lot of effort had to go into the planning. Chalky, Dawkins and I rehearsed several times, and we spent hours working out who would stand where. We eventually put numbers on the floor to mark their places. First we had to photograph the wedding group and their guests from the royal houses of Europe, fifty-seven in all. I used a whistle to attract everybody's attention. The result is a picture of which I'm quite proud. Nobody is hidden, and everybody is looking at the camera.

Front row, left to right: Edward van Cutsem, the Earl of Ulster, Catherine Cameron, Clementine Hambro, Sarah-Jane Gaselee, Lord Nicholas Windsor.

Second row: King Carl Gustav and Queen Silvia of Sweden, King Baudouin and Queen Fabiola of Belgium, Princess Margaret, Princess Anne, Queen Elizabeth the Queen Mother, The Queen, India Hicks, Lady Sarah Armstrong-Jones, the Hon Mrs Shand Kydd, Earl Spencer, Lady Sarah McCorquodale, Neil McCorquodale, Queen Beatrix of the Netherlands, Lady Helen Windsor, Grand Duke Jean and Grand Duchess Josephine Charlotte of Luxembourg.

Third row: Prince Henrik and Queen Margrethe of Denmark, King Olav of Norway, James and Marina Ogilvy, Captain Mark Phillips, the Hon Angus Ogilvy, Princess Alexandra, Prince Andrew, Viscount Linley, the Duchess of Gloucester, Prince Philip, the Duke of Gloucester, Prince Edward, Princess Alice, the Princess of Wales, the Duke of Kent, Ruth, Lady Fermoy, the Prince of Wales, the Earl of St Andrews, the Duchess of Kent, Viscount Althorp, Lady Jane Fellowes, Robert Fellowes, Prince Michael of Kent, Princess Michael of Kent, Princess Grace of Monaco, Prince Claus of the Netherlands, Prince Albert of Monaco, Princess Gina and Prince Franz Josef of Liechtenstein.

Queen Elizabeth went to Badminton in April 1982. I chose this picture because it is so characteristic of Her Majesty. She is really happiest in the fresh air watching horses, either racing or eventing. She is never daunted by the weather, and in fact relishes wet and windy days. However, for the increased comfort of other spectators, and of course the competitors, the Badminton three-day event has been moved to the warmer month of May since the death of the old Duke of Beaufort.

Queen Elizabeth, the Princess of Wales, Princess Alice of Gloucester and King Olav of Norway look down from the balcony of the old Home Office at the Cenotaph, London, on Remembrance Sunday, 8th November 1981. Queen Elizabeth herself contributes a wreath each year which is laid for her. The Royal British Legion organizes several events around Remembrance Sunday. A few days before there is a gathering at the Field of Remembrance at St Margaret's Westminster, and Queen Elizabeth has attended this to plant a wooden cross almost every year since the death of George VI. There is also a colourful spectacle at the Royal Albert Hall on the Saturday evening at which members of the royal family are always present.

Prince William's christening took place on Queen Elizabeth's 82nd birthday. It was held in the Music Room, which since the loss of the chapel during the war has taken over Buckingham Palace's religious duties. Other babies who have been christened there include Prince Charles, Princess Anne, Prince Andrew and Princess Anne's son Peter Phillips. It was the Archbishop of Canterbury, Dr Runcie's first royal christening. The baby was named William Arthur Philip Louis. William was chosen, stressed Prince Charles, because he and the Princess Diana like the name. If he lives as long as his great grandmother he will be present at the great anniversary of his namesake, William the Conqueror's millenium in the year 2066. Arthur, one of Prince Charles's names, was after one of the Queen's godfathers, Prince Arthur, Duke of Connaught. He in turn, who was Queen Victoria's third son, was named after his own grandfather the Duke of Wellington, Arthur Wellesley, who won at Waterloo. Philip is from Prince William's grandfather, and Louis is after Earl Mountbatten of Burma, Prince Philip's uncle.

Queen Elizabeth sits surrounded by four of her grandchildren, Prince Charles, Princess Anne, Prince Andrew and Prince Edward, taken by Norman Parkinson for her eighty-fifth birthday. Like the eightieth birthday portrait through the window, the use of back lighting makes this picture work, though here it is more subtle. On the great day itself she went to Kings Lynn to hear the Russian cellist Rostropovitch. However, she was in London next day to make a walkabout amongst the 2,000 well-wishers who had gathered. As a birthday present the chairman of British Airways gave her a trip around Britain in Concorde. As they passed over Glamis at 66,000 feet she ate lunch with her other grandchildren Viscount Linley and Lady Armstrong-Jones. She had first expressed an interest in making such a trip when the aeroplane was still undergoing trials and hadn't even been granted its certificate of airworthiness.

Queen Elizabeth at the Castle of Mey in 1983. She is usually in residence at her favourite home on the Pentland Firth during July and August. Despite being so far north the weather is surprisingly temperate, though blustery is an understatement. It's a beautiful little castle, which has responded well to her careful restoration and decoration. Quite often, other members of the royal family go cruising in the Western Isles aboard *Britannia*, and they will always find time to put into the Firth and visit Queen Elizabeth. It is also a relatively short helicopter flight to Balmoral.

The Black Watch celebrated its 125th anniversary in 1987, and Queen Elizabeth went to Montreal to inspect the guard of honour of Canada's Royal Highland Regiment. She is their Colonel-in-Chief. She is here accompanied by Lt. Col. Victor Chartier, their commanding officer. During her four day visit to Canada she also went to Quebec, becoming the first member of the royal family to visit the city since the Queen opened the Montreal Olympics there in 1976. She was received by the Governor-General, Mme Jeanne Sauve, and the Prime Minister and his wife, Brian and Mila Mulroney.

Opposite: Whenever possible Queen Elizabeth attends the annual service of the Friends of St Paul's Cathedral. This lovely picture shows Her Majesty being received at the Cathedral on 13th July 1988. She is shaking hands with Canon Peter Ball, watched appreciatively by Canon Graham Routledge (who died the following year), Bishop Kenneth Woolcombe, and the Dean of St Paul's the Very Reverend Eric Evans.

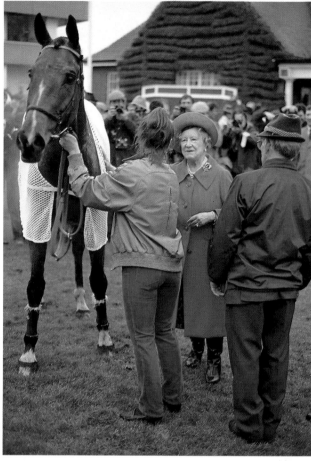

Queen Elizabeth at Westminster Abbey on 9th February 1989. Prince Charles has written of her: 'I would have said that most grandsons probably have a rather special relationship with their grandmothers, which is no doubt something to do with the difference in generations, but ever since I can remember my grandmother has been the most wonderful example of fun, laughter, warmth, infinite security and, above all else, exquisite taste in so many things. For me, she has always been one of those extraordinarily rare people whose touch can turn anything to gold – whether it be putting people at their ease, turning something dull into something amusing, bringing happiness and comfort to people by her presence or making any house she lives in a unique haven of cosiness and character. She belongs to that priceless brand of human beings whose greatest gift is to enhance life for others through her own effervescent enthusiasm for life.'

Queen Elizabeth at Sandown races with the horse Sun Rising who carried her colours on 10th March 1989. Sun Rising, the favourite, was beaten into second place by a neck in the three-mile Grand Military Gold Cup by Brother Geoffrey. The Princess Royal came third in the same race on her horse Bobby Kelly. Queen Elizabeth no longer has as many horses as she used to, but she doesn't play the game for money. She doesn't even bet. A retired horse from her stable won't be sold, and Devon Loch spent his declining days munching through the Sandringham grass. Her colours in National Hunt racing are pale blue shirt and sleeves, buff stripes, and a black hat with a gold tassell. Queen Elizabeth comes from a long tradition 'over the sticks'. Her grandfather, the 13th Earl of Strathmore had been a great racehorse owner, and a cousin, John Bowes, won the Derby four times. She herself, became patron of the National Hunt Committee and of the Injured Jockey's Fund.

Opposite: Queen Elizabeth at the Field of Remembrance, St Margaret's Westminster, on 11th November 1989. Every year she joins veterans of the British Legion, who draw as much inspiration from her today as they did fifty years ago.

Opposite: This arresting picture of Queen Elizabeth, the Princess of Wales and Princess Anne carrying identical posies of roses and gypsophila was taken at the première of Sir David Lean's film A Passage to India on 18th March 1985. Although the royal family frequently attend premières it is certainly unusual to see such a large royal turnout, especially since this wasn't a command performance. One thing these three ladies have in common is their enormous work for charity. Princess Anne had just returned from a gruelling tour of Calcutta, Madras and New Delhi, on behalf of the Save the Children Fund. The Princess of Wales was shortly to leave for Italy where she met the Pope and visited the Hospital of Baby Jesus in Florence, the Italian equivalent of the Great Ormonde Street Hospital for sick children, of which she is Patron.

Queen Elizabeth on her eighty-ninth birthday at Clarence House clutching flags and flowers. Her lifelong friend Lord Cecil once said: 'Her sense of duty and patriotism are helped by her dramatic sense. She thinks she *ought* to wave and give pleasure. And she is able to perform these feelings to the public. Others might have the gift, but suffer from the wrong friends – dreary advisers – while this gift can make some people unreliable, like Edward VIII. Hers is an honourable and simple view of life. She has been able to put it across to the millions because of this gift of performance.'

Acknowledgements The author, producer and editor acknowledge substantial help with the preparation of this book from a number of people. Particular thanks are due to Major John Griffin MVO and his assistant, Lucy Murphy, at Clarence House; the staff of the Hulton Deutsch Collection, notably Peter Elliott and Roger Wemyss-Brooks, who instigated the project, and John Chillingworth, Milica Timotic, Carl Newell and Mathew Butson who have helped with the pictures. Liz Belton, Peter Fitzmaurice, Venetia Hesketh-Prichard, Nell Jacoby, Elizabeth Kerry, Philip Way, R.E. Wilson MVO, and Michelle Wilson have all given vital assistance, and, on the production side, so have Mike Ersser, Philip Chippindale and Suthep Taithongchai. We are grateful to them all.